THE KINGFISHER
First
Picture Atlas

Written by Deborah Chancellor

Illustrated by Anthony Lewis

KINGFISHER

KINGFISHER

First published in 2005 by Kingfisher
an imprint of Macmillan Children's Books
a division of Macmillan Publishers Limited
20 New Wharf Road, London N1 9RR
Basingstoke and Oxford
Associated compaines throughout the world
www.panmacmillan.com

Consultant: Keith Lye

ISBN 978-0-7534-3310-2

Copyright © Macmillan Children's Books 2005

10 9 8 7 6 5 4 3 2 1
1TF/0111/WKT/CLSN/105MA

A CIP catalogue record is available for this book
from the British Library.

Printed in China

CREDITS
The Publisher would like to thank the following for permission
to reproduce their material. Every care has been taken to trace copyright
holders. However, if there have been unintentional omissions or failure to
trace copyright holders, we apologise and will, if informed, endeavour to
make corrections in any future edition.

2 NASA; 7 Corbis/Galen Rowell; 8 Corbis/Yann Arthus-Bertrand; 13
Photolibrary/Walter Bibikow; 15 Alamy/Robert Harding Picture Library;
16 Alamy/Bob Turner; 19 Alamy/ Robert Harding Picture Library; 20
Alamy/Imagestate; 22 Alamy/Andre Jenny; 24 Alamy/Mervyn Rees; 27
Corbis/ Reuters; 28 Getty/311214-001; 30 Corbis/Arko Datta/Reuters;
32 Alamy/SC Photos; 35 Alamy/Worldwide Pic Lib; 37 Photolibrary/John
Downer; 38 Corbis/Yann Arthus-Bertrand; 41 Alamy/Robert Harding
Picture Library; 42 Rex; 43 Getty/Stone; 45 Alamy/Nordicphotos

Contents

About the earth

The earth is a planet in space. It is shaped like a ball and is covered with land and sea. Photographs can show us what the earth looks like. Maps help us understand more about the world.

Countries of the world

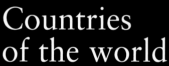

A country (such as Italy, map above) is a part of the world with its own people and laws. There are around 200 countries in the world. The number changes if countries break up or join together in new ways.

Continents

A continent is a huge mass of land. Some continents, such as South America (map above), contain many different countries. On maps of continents, lines are drawn to show the borders between countries. You cannot see these lines on a photograph, because they are not really there.

What is a map?

A map is a picture of the earth that shows natural and man-made features. A globe is a kind of map that is in the shape of a ball, just like the earth itself. We cannot see the whole world at once on a globe. If we want to do this, we need to look at a flat map.

Making a map

To make a flat map, the globe is split into segments, and 'peeled' like an orange.

The segments are then placed side by side.

These segments are used to create a flat map (see the map of the world on page 10).

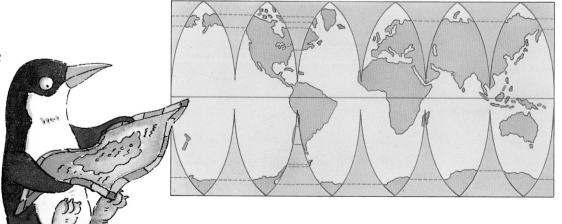

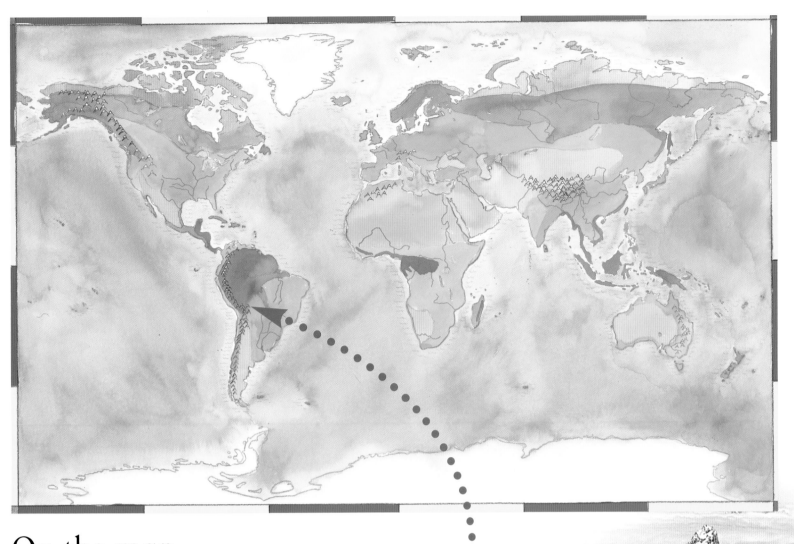

On the map

Most maps show the curved surface of the earth on a flat piece of paper. Map-makers have to change the shape of some countries and oceans to fit them together on a flat map.

Showing mountains

Special colours and symbols on maps show us where to find important features of the landscape, such as these beautiful mountains in South America.

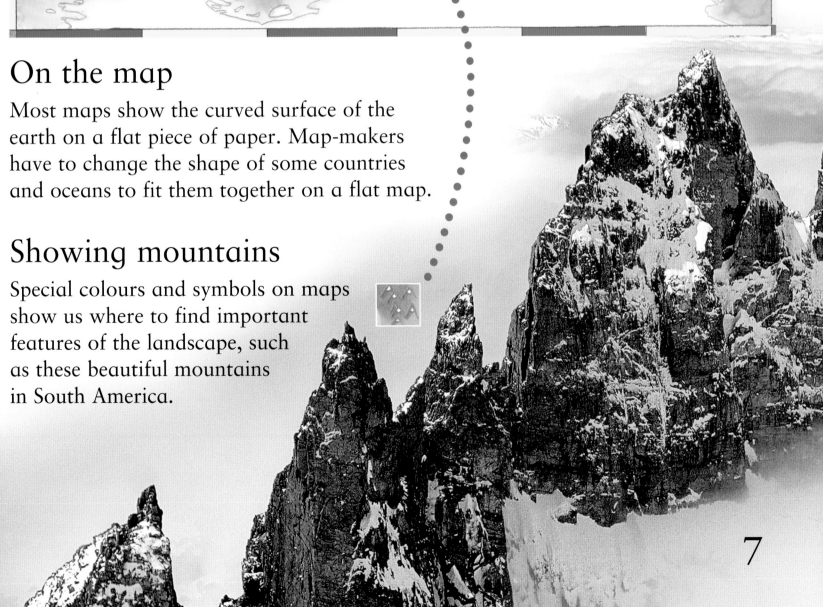

Using an atlas

An atlas is a book of maps. To use an atlas, you need to understand how maps work. Maps are much smaller than the places they show. They have lots of information in a very small space.

Pictures show industries, animals or landmarks.

Grid band 'C'

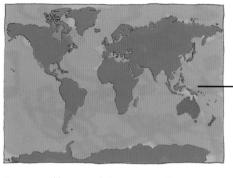

A small world map shows you where to find the countries shown on the main map.

Grid band '2'

A grid helps you find places on the map. Here, Alice Springs is in square C2. You can find this by tracing your finger down from the letter C band and across from the number 2 band.

In this atlas, a story box picks out an interesting fact.

Gulf of Carpentaria

Darwin

Seahorse

Aboriginal cave painting

NORTHERN TERRITORY

Great Sandy Desert

TROPIC OF CAPRICORN

Mining

Gibson Desert

A U S T R A L I

Alice Springs

Simpson Desert

SOUTH AUSTRALIA

WESTERN AUSTRALIA

Kangaroo

Lake Eyre

Great Victoria Desert

The Ghan

Perth

Farming

Great Australian Bight

Adelaide

Great white shark

Uluru is a sandstone monolith rising high above the desert in Australia's Northern Territory. It is the largest rock of its kind in the world.

Look for the star ✹

38

Map key

Colours, lines and symbols on maps stand for many different things. These details are explained in a key to the map. In this atlas, the key helps you find cities, borders and rivers. It also shows what the colours on the map mean.

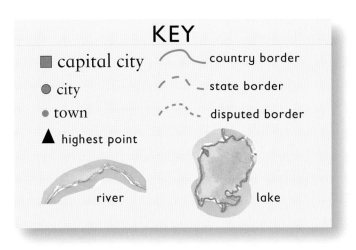

KEY

- ■ capital city
- ● city
- ● town
- ▲ highest point
- ~~~ country border
- ‐‐‐ state border
- ·‐·‐ disputed border
- river
- lake

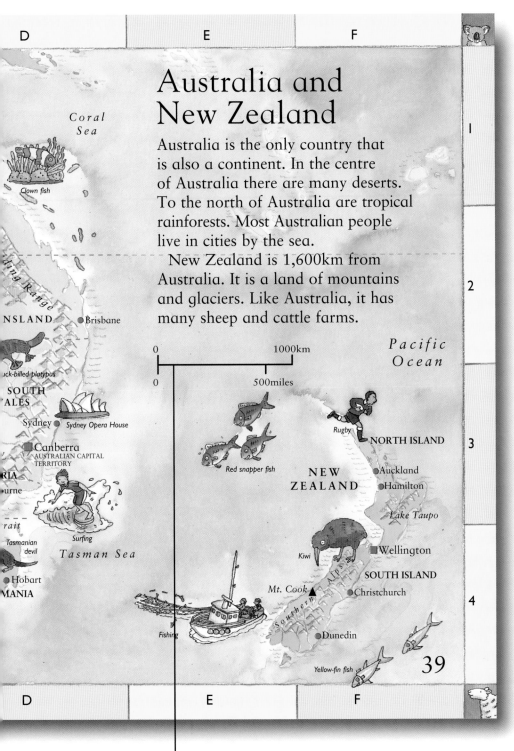

Australia and New Zealand

Australia is the only country that is also a continent. In the centre of Australia there are many deserts. To the north of Australia are tropical rainforests. Most Australian people live in cities by the sea.

New Zealand is 1,600km from Australia. It is a land of mountains and glaciers. Like Australia, it has many sheep and cattle farms.

Coral Sea

Clown fish

uck-billed platypus

NSLAND • Brisbane

SOUTH ALES

Sydney ● • Sydney Opera House

■ Canberra
AUSTRALIAN CAPITAL TERRITORY

RIA

urne

rait

Tasmanian devil

Tasman Sea

Surfing

● Hobart

MANIA

0   1000km

0   500miles

Red snapper fish

Rugby

NORTH ISLAND

NEW ZEALAND

● Auckland

● Hamilton

Lake Taupo

Kiwi

■ Wellington

SOUTH ISLAND

Mt. Cook ▲

● Christchurch

Southern Alps

Fishing

● Dunedin

Pacific Ocean

Yellow-fin fish

39

Desert Dry areas with few plants, often sandy and rocky

Dry grassland Flat, grassy plains with only a few trees

Temperate grassland Flat, grassy plains with some trees

Forest Areas with lots of trees

Mountains Tall hills and rugged landscape

Tundra Flat area near Arctic with frozen ground and no trees

Ice and snow Places where ice and snow cover the ground

Seas and oceans Salty water that covers much of the earth

A scale bar helps you understand how big areas are on the map.

NORTH
AMERICA

*Atlantic
Ocean*

*Pacific
Ocean*

SOUTH
AMERICA

*Atlantic
Ocean*

The world

Maps of the world show the seven
continents. All the continents, except
Antarctica and Australia, are made
up of many different countries.
Lines are drawn on world maps
that do not exist on the ground,
for example the Equator and the
Tropics of Cancer and Capricorn.

PRIME
MERIDIAN

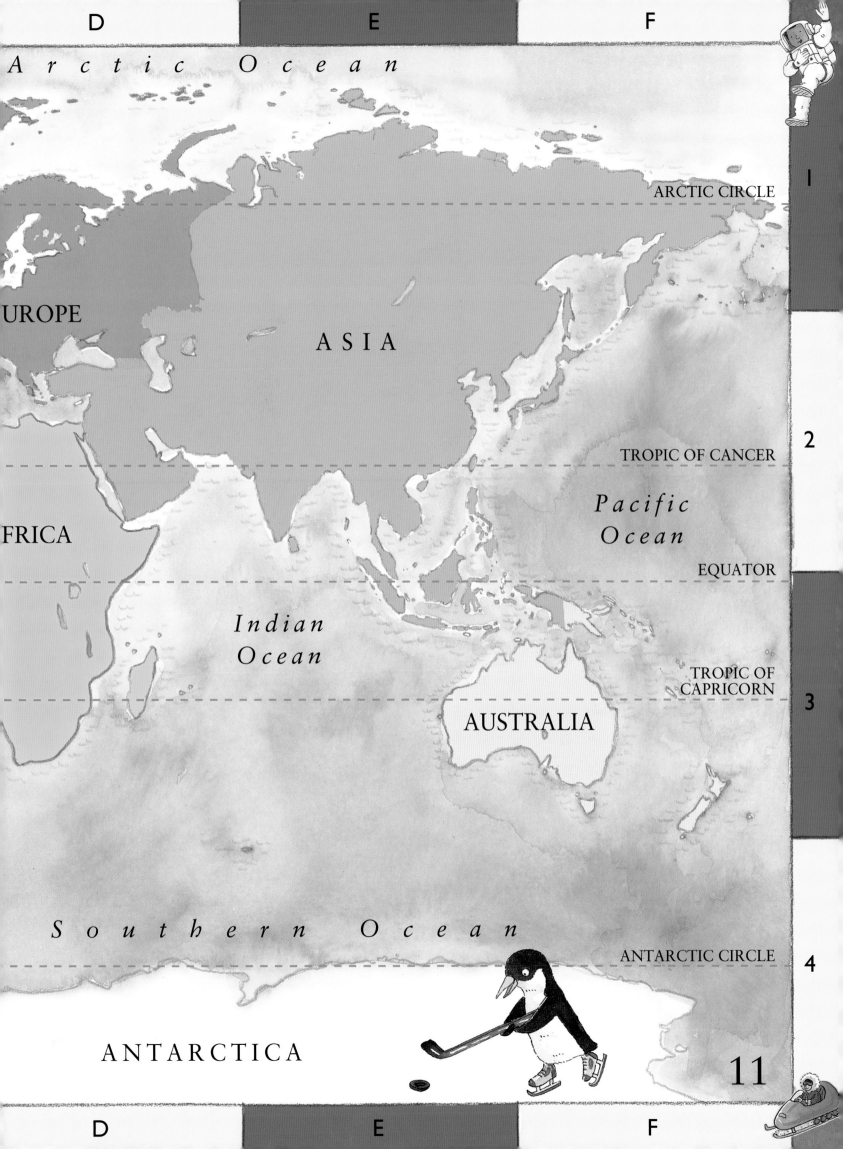

Arctic Ocean

ARCTIC CIRCLE

1

UROPE

ASIA

TROPIC OF CANCER

2

FRICA

Pacific Ocean

EQUATOR

Indian Ocean

TROPIC OF CAPRICORN

3

AUSTRALIA

Southern Ocean

ANTARCTIC CIRCLE

4

ANTARCTICA

11

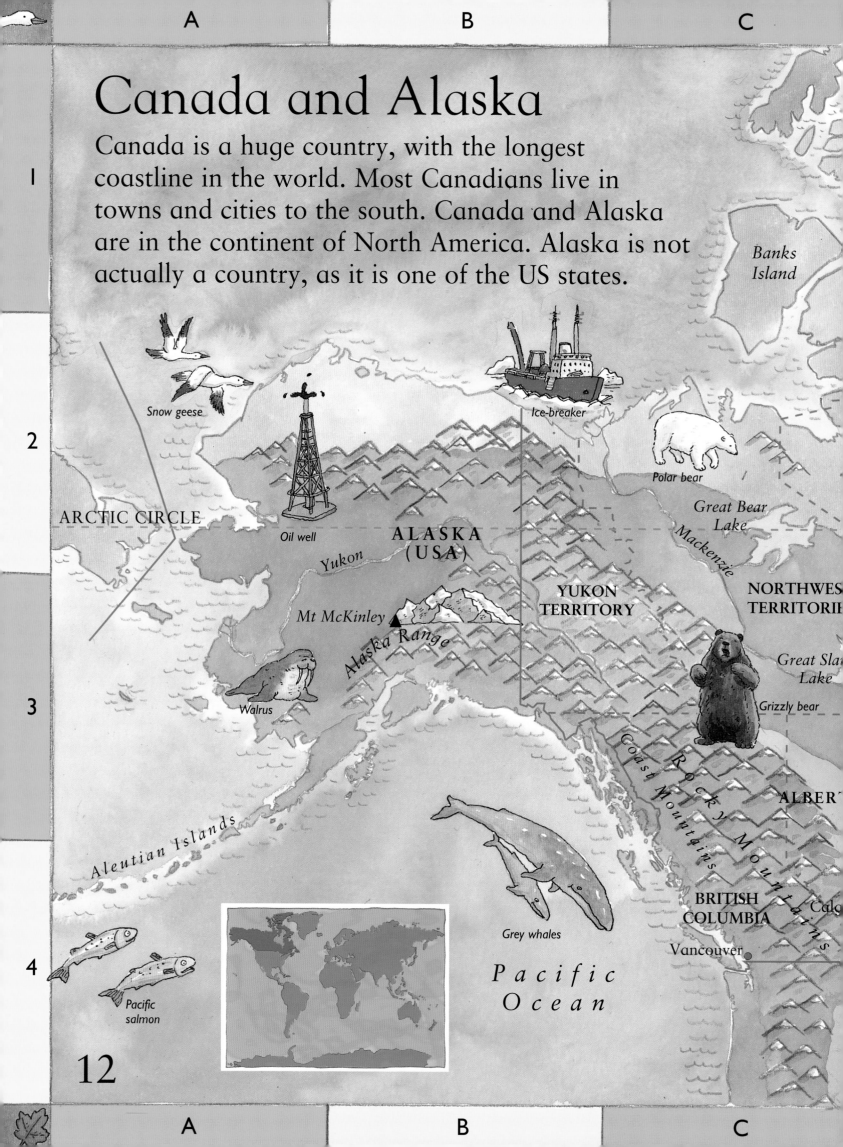

Canada and Alaska

Canada is a huge country, with the longest coastline in the world. Most Canadians live in towns and cities to the south. Canada and Alaska are in the continent of North America. Alaska is not actually a country, as it is one of the US states.

A   B   C

Banks Island

Snow geese

Ice-breaker

Polar bear

ARCTIC CIRCLE

Oil well

ALASKA (USA)

Yukon

Great Bear Lake

Mackenzie

YUKON TERRITORY

NORTHWEST TERRITORIES

Mt McKinley

Alaska Range

Great Slave Lake

Grizzly bear

Walrus

Coast Mountains

Rocky Mountains

ALBERTA

Aleutian Islands

BRITISH COLUMBIA

Calgary

Vancouver

Grey whales

Pacific Ocean

Pacific salmon

12

en Elizabeth Islands

Ellesmere
Island

Devon
Island

Victoria
Island

Québec is the only walled
city in North America. It
was founded in 1608 on
the banks of the mighty
St Lawrence river.

Look for the star ✴

Baffin
Island

NUNAVUT

ARCTIC CIRCLE

Reindeer

Inuit

Lake
Athabasca

*H u d s o n
B a y*

Iceberg

*A t l a n t i c
O c e a n*

MANITOBA

SASKATCHEWAN

C A N A D A

Lake
Winnipeg

Timber industry

Skier

QUEBEC

NEWFOUNDLAND
AND LABRADOR

Arable farming

ONTARIO

Lake
Superior

Toronto's
CN Tower

Industry

St Lawrence

NEW
BRUNSWICK

1000km

Lake
Huron

Québec

Montreal

Ottawa

Lake Ontario

PRINCE
EDWARD
ISLAND

500 miles

Lake Erie

NOVA SCOTIA

13

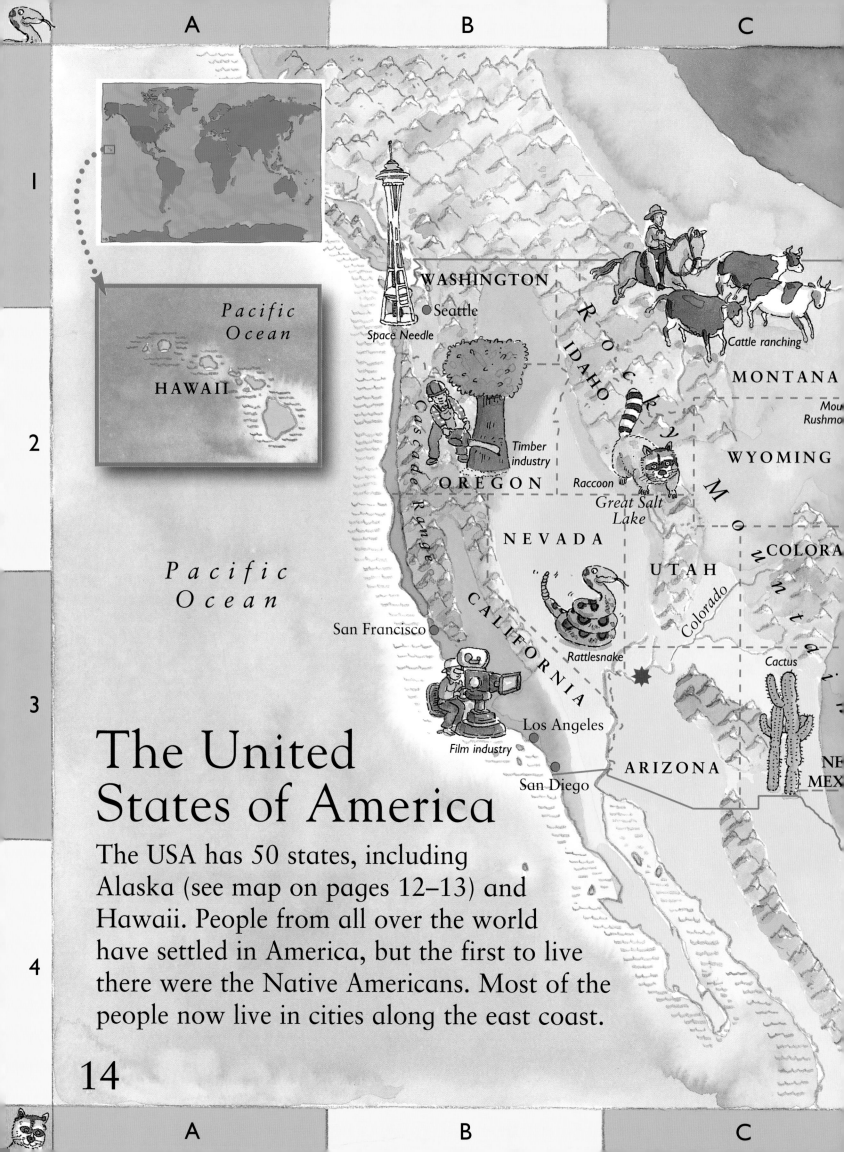

Pacific Ocean

HAWAII

Pacific Ocean

WASHINGTON

• Seattle

Space Needle

ROCKY

IDAHO

Cattle ranching

MONTANA

Mount Rushmore

Timber industry

OREGON

Raccoon

WYOMING

Great Salt Lake

NEVADA

UTAH

COLORADO

Mountains

San Francisco

CALIFORNIA

Rattlesnake

Colorado

Cactus

Film industry

Los Angeles

ARIZONA

NEW MEXICO

San Diego

The United States of America

The USA has 50 states, including Alaska (see map on pages 12–13) and Hawaii. People from all over the world have settled in America, but the first to live there were the Native Americans. Most of the people now live in cities along the east coast.

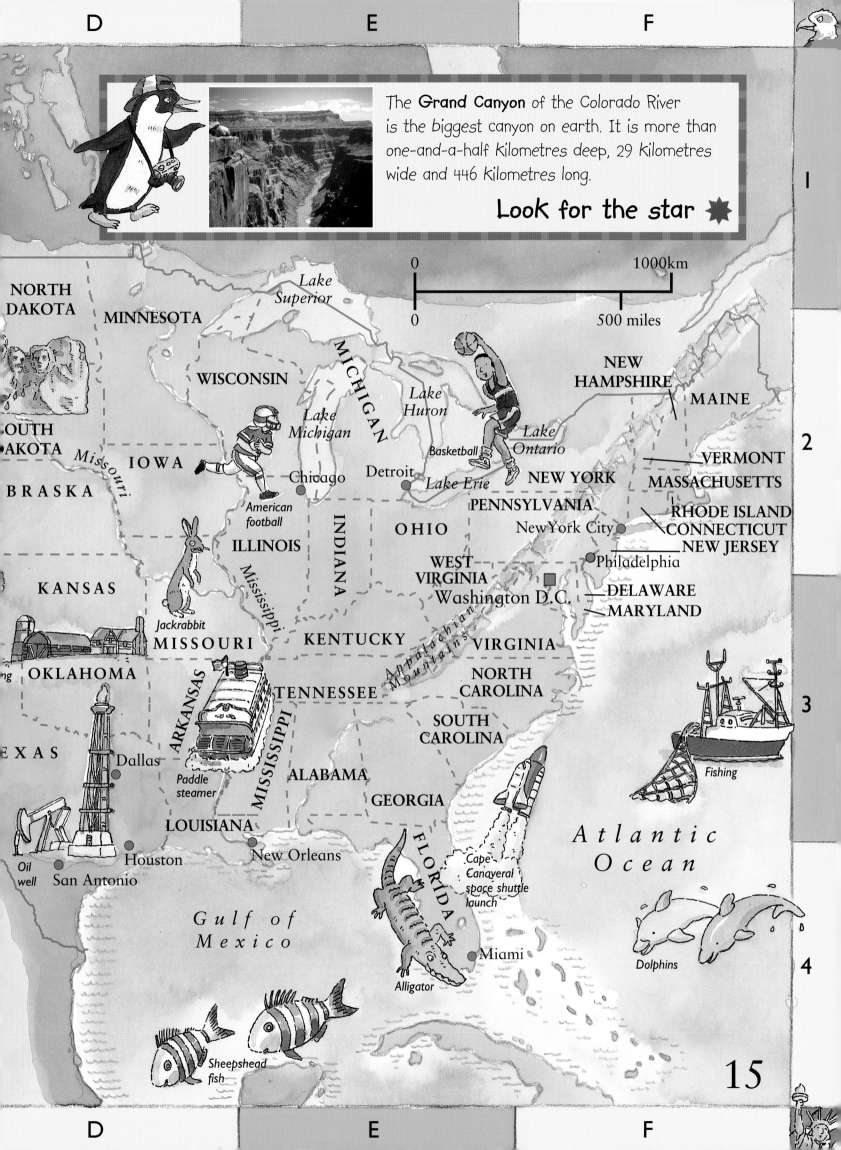

The **Grand Canyon** of the Colorado River is the biggest canyon on earth. It is more than one-and-a-half kilometres deep, 29 Kilometres wide and 446 Kilometres long.

Look for the star ✶

0   1000km

0   500 miles

NORTH DAKOTA

MINNESOTA

Lake Superior

MICHIGAN

NEW HAMPSHIRE

WISCONSIN

Lake Huron

MAINE

Lake Michigan

SOUTH DAKOTA

IOWA

Detroit

Basketball

Lake Ontario

NEW YORK

VERMONT

MASSACHUSETTS

BRASKA

Chicago

Lake Erie

PENNSYLVANIA

American football

NewYork City

RHODE ISLAND
CONNECTICUT
NEW JERSEY

ILLINOIS

INDIANA

OHIO

Philadelphia

KANSAS

Mississippi

WEST VIRGINIA

Washington D.C.

DELAWARE

MARYLAND

Jackrabbit

KENTUCKY

VIRGINIA

Missouri

MISSOURI

Appalachian Mountains

OKLAHOMA

NORTH CAROLINA

ARKANSAS

TENNESSEE

SOUTH CAROLINA

EXAS

Dallas

Paddle steamer

MISSISSIPPI

ALABAMA

Fishing

GEORGIA

Houston

Oil well

San Antonio

LOUISIANA

New Orleans

FLORIDA

Cape Canaveral space shuttle launch

Atlantic Ocean

Gulf of Mexico

Miami

Dolphins

Alligator

Sheepshead fish

15

1

2

3

4

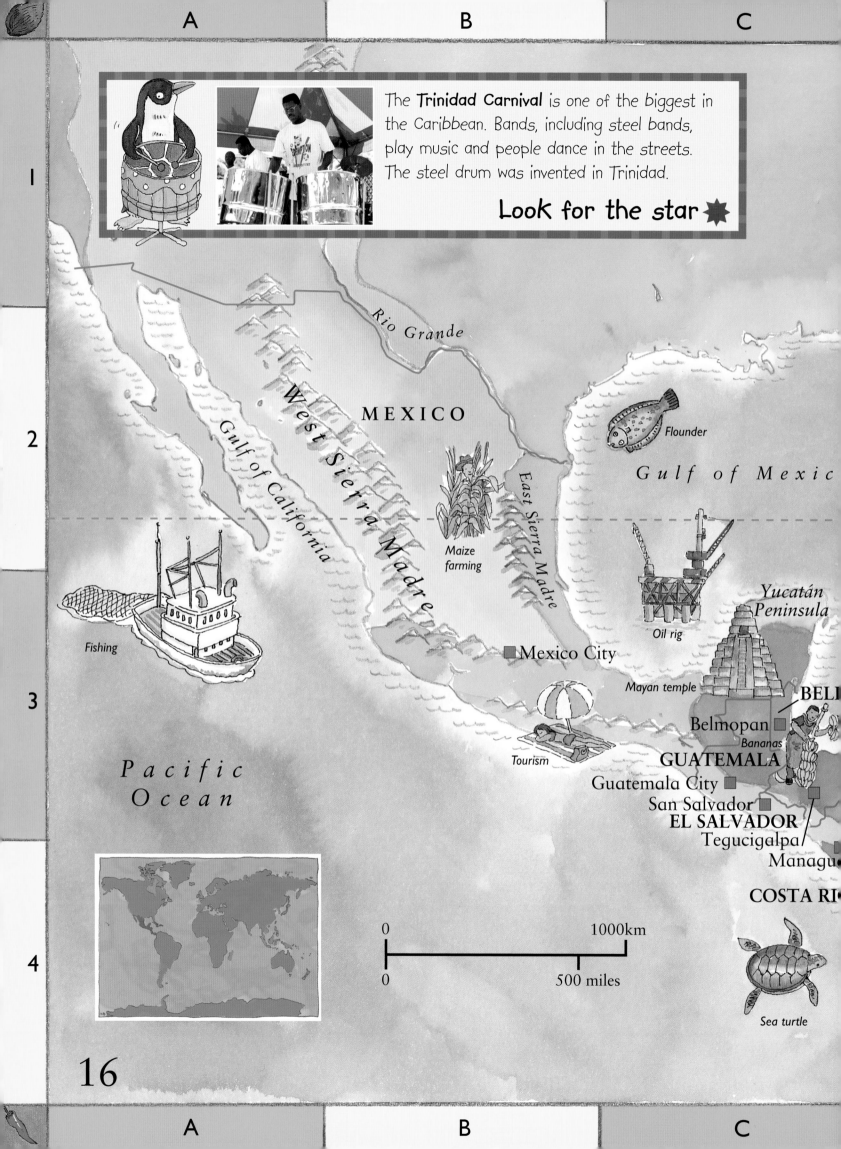

The **Trinidad Carnival** is one of the biggest in the Caribbean. Bands, including steel bands, play music and people dance in the streets. The steel drum was invented in Trinidad.

Look for the star ✹

1

Rio Grande

MEXICO

West Sierra Madre

Gulf of California

East Sierra Madre

Flounder

2

Gulf of Mexic

Maize farming

Oil rig

Yucatán Peninsula

Mexico City

Mayan temple

BELI

Fishing

3

Belmopan

Bananas

GUATEMALA

Tourism

Guatemala City

San Salvador

Pacific Ocean

EL SALVADOR

Tegucigalpa

Managu

COSTA RI

0   1000km

0   500 miles

4

Sea turtle

16

Mexico, Central America and the Caribbean

Mexico, Central America and the Caribbean
islands are in the continent of North America.
Mexico is the largest country in the region.
The islands of the Caribbean are countries too.
More than half of all Caribbean people live
in Cuba and the Dominican Republic.

Palm tree

BAHAMAS
◼ Nassau

TROPIC OF CANCER

◼ Havana

Coral reef

Scuba diving

*A t l a n t i c
O c e a n*

CUBA

**DOMINICAN
REPUBLIC**

HAITI

PUERTO RICO (USA)
◼ San Juan

Sugar cane

JAMAICA ◼

◼ Port-au-
Prince

◼ Santo
Domingo

**ST KITTS &
NEVIS**

ANTIGUA & BARBUDA

Kingston

**DOMINICA
ST LUCIA**

NDURAS

C a r i b b e a n   S e a

**ST VINCENT &
THE GRENADINES
BARBADOS**

ARAGUA

GRENADA

José

Panama Canal

Spotfin butterfly fish

◼ Port-of-Spain
**TRINIDAD &
TOBAGO**

◼ Panama City

ANAMA

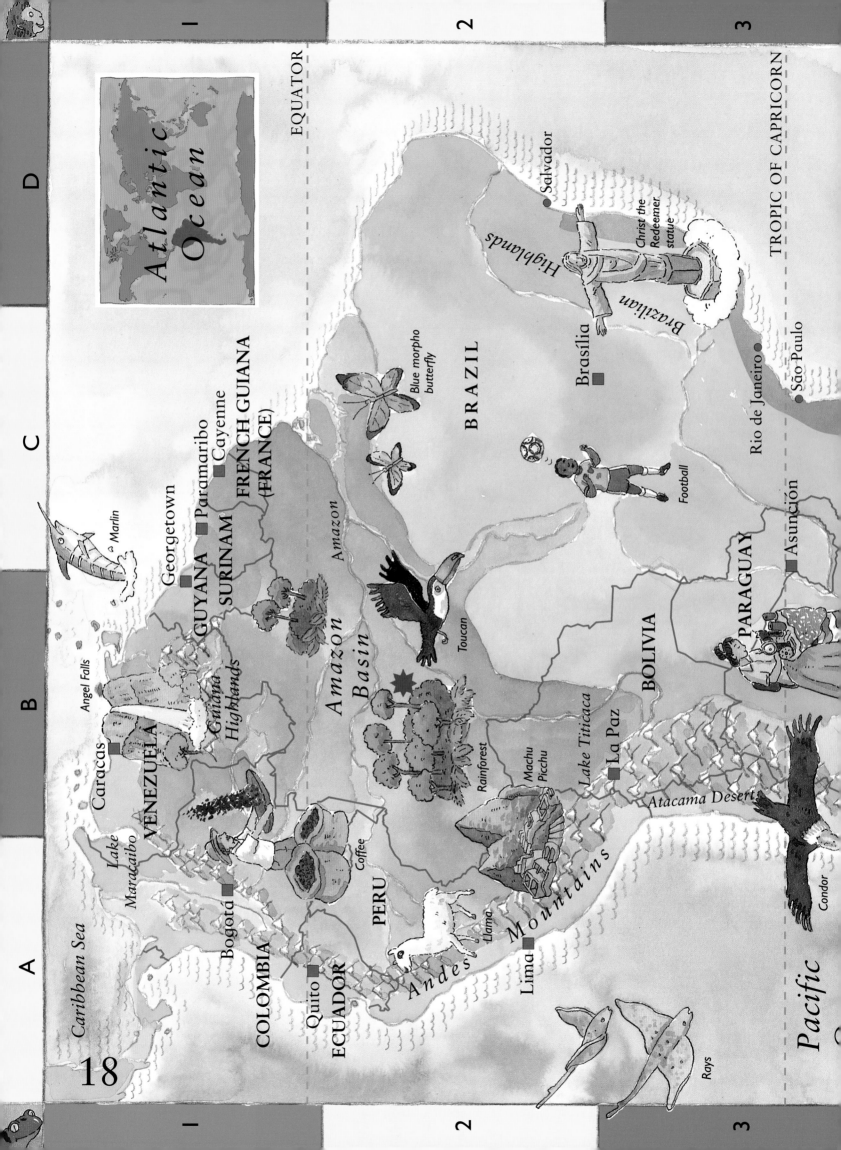

Caribbean Sea

Atlantic Ocean

EQUATOR

TROPIC OF CAPRICORN

Marlin

Angel Falls

Georgetown

GUYANA

Paramaribo

SURINAM

Cayenne

FRENCH GUIANA
(FRANCE)

Guiana
Highlands

Blue morpho
butterfly

Lake
Maracaibo

Caracas

VENEZUELA

Bogotá

COLOMBIA

Amazon

Amazon
Basin

Toucan

BRAZIL

Highlands

Brazilian

Salvador

Brasília

Christ the
Redeemer
statue

Quito

ECUADOR

Coffee

PERU

Rainforest

Llama

Machu
Picchu

Lake Titicaca

La Paz

BOLIVIA

Football

Rio de Janeiro

São Paulo

Lima

Andes Mountains

Atacama Desert

PARAGUAY

Asunción

Pacific

Rays

Condor

South America

South America is a continent of extremes. Tall, snowy mountains lie to the west, while the steamy Amazon rainforest covers a huge area to the north. The southern tip of the continent is very dry and freezing cold.

Aeroplane

Santé Fé

URUGUAY
■ Montevideo

Paraná

ARGENTINA
■ Buenos Aires

Mt Aconcagua
■ Santiago
CHILE
Concepción ●

Grapes

Andes Mount

Sheep farming

Patagonia

Oil rig

FALKLAND ISLANDS (UK)
■ Stanley

Cape Horn

Sardines

Fishing

1000km
500 miles
0
0

The **Amazon rainforest** contains about half of all the animal and plant species in the world. Many are still waiting to be discovered.

★ Look for the star

19

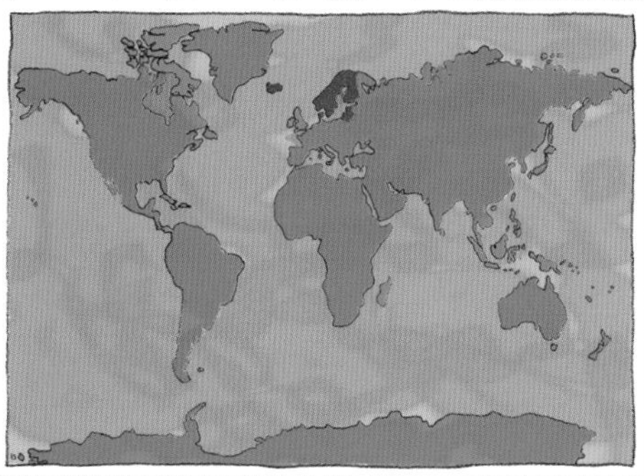

Northern Europe

Forests, lakes and mountains cover large parts of northern Europe. The countries Norway, Sweden and Denmark make up a region called Scandinavia. To the east lies Finland. South of the Baltic Sea are the small countries of Estonia, Latvia and Lithuania.

ARCTIC CIRCLE

ICELAND

Geyser
■ Reykjavik

Cod

Iceland cat shark

Fishing

A t l a n t i c
O c e a n

Nor
Se

Hans Christian Andersen, the famous children's writer, lived in Denmark. A statue of his Little Mermaid is in Copenhagen, the Danish capital city.

Look for the star ✴

PRIME MERIDIAN 0°

400km

200 miles

Hammerfest

L a p l a n d

Kiruna

Arctic fox

Fjord

Fishing

Pine forest

ARCTIC CIRCLE

Reindeer and Sami

Norwegian Sea

FINLAND

Oulu

Lake Oulujärvi

SWEDEN

Oil rig

Trondheim

Pine forest

Paper mills

L a k e   r e g i o n

Gulf of Bothnia

NORWAY

ergen

Åland

Helsinki

Oslo

Industry

Gulf of Finland

Stockholm

Baltic Sea

Tallinn

Lake Vänern

ESTONIA

Lake Vättern

Göteborg

Gotland

LATVIA

Ríga

DENMARK

Pig farming

Cattle farming

Copenhagen

Lego

LITHUANIA

Vilnius

Western Europe

Much of the land in western Europe is used for farming. Industries, such as car factories, are also important. Some cities are very old, and attract many tourists. Countries around the Mediterranean Sea are very hot in summer.

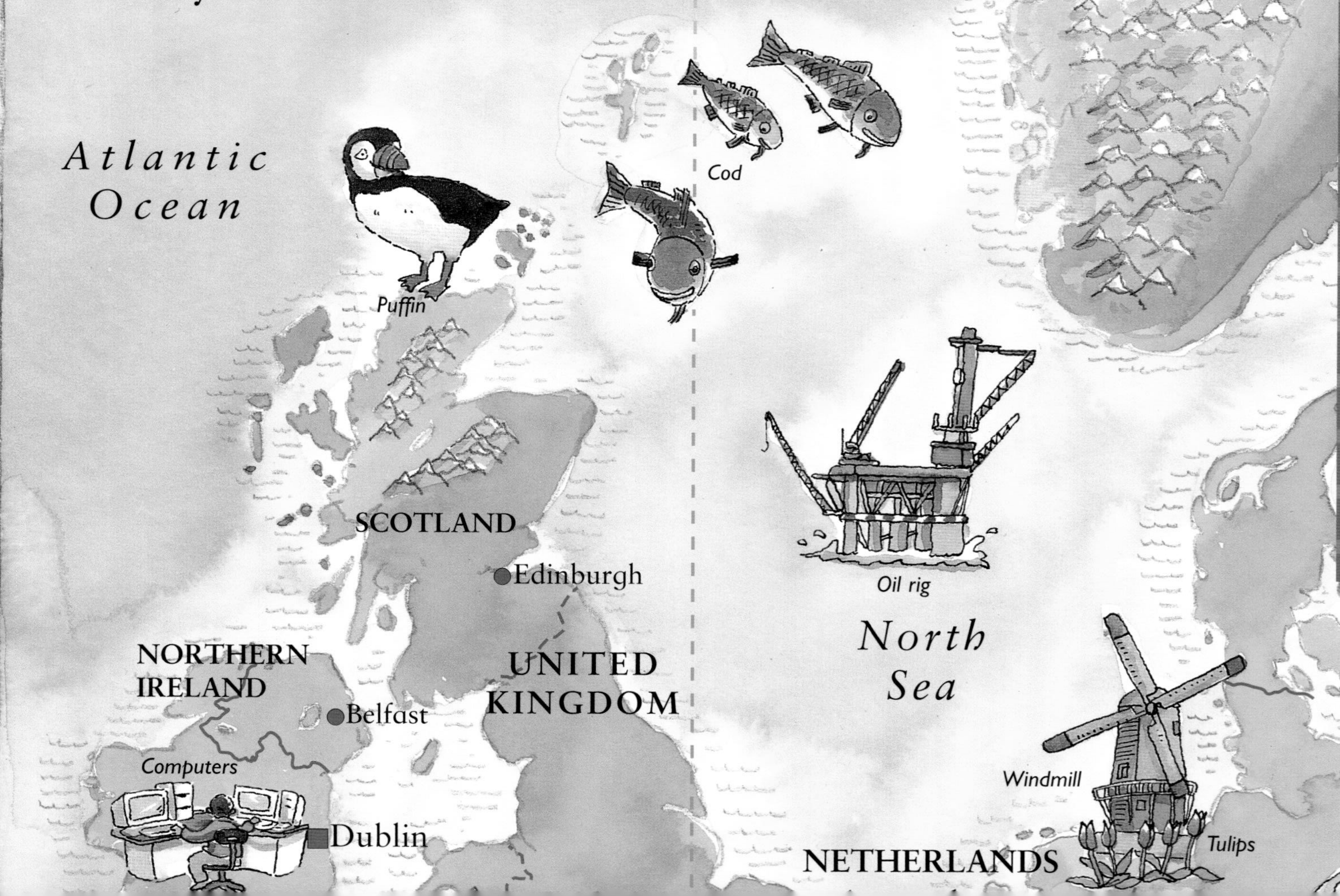

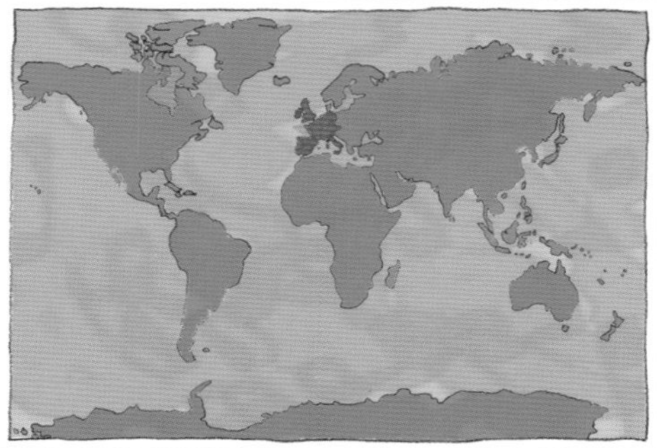

France's most famous landmark, the **Eiffel Tower**, sways up to 12cm from side to side in high winds.

Look for the star

Baltic Sea

Atlantic Ocean

Puffin

Cod

Oil rig

North Sea

Windmill

Tulips

Car industry

NETHERLANDS

SCOTLAND

●Edinburgh

UNITED KINGDOM

NORTHERN IRELAND

●Belfast

Dublin

Computers

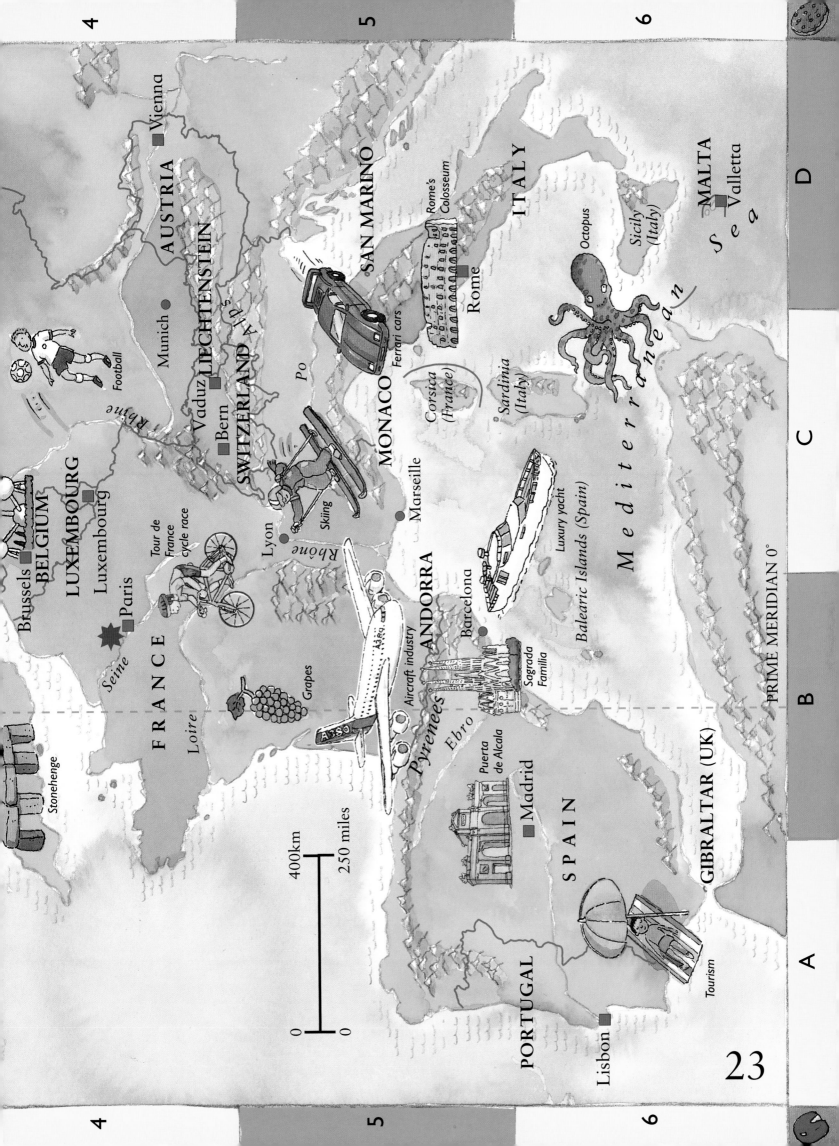

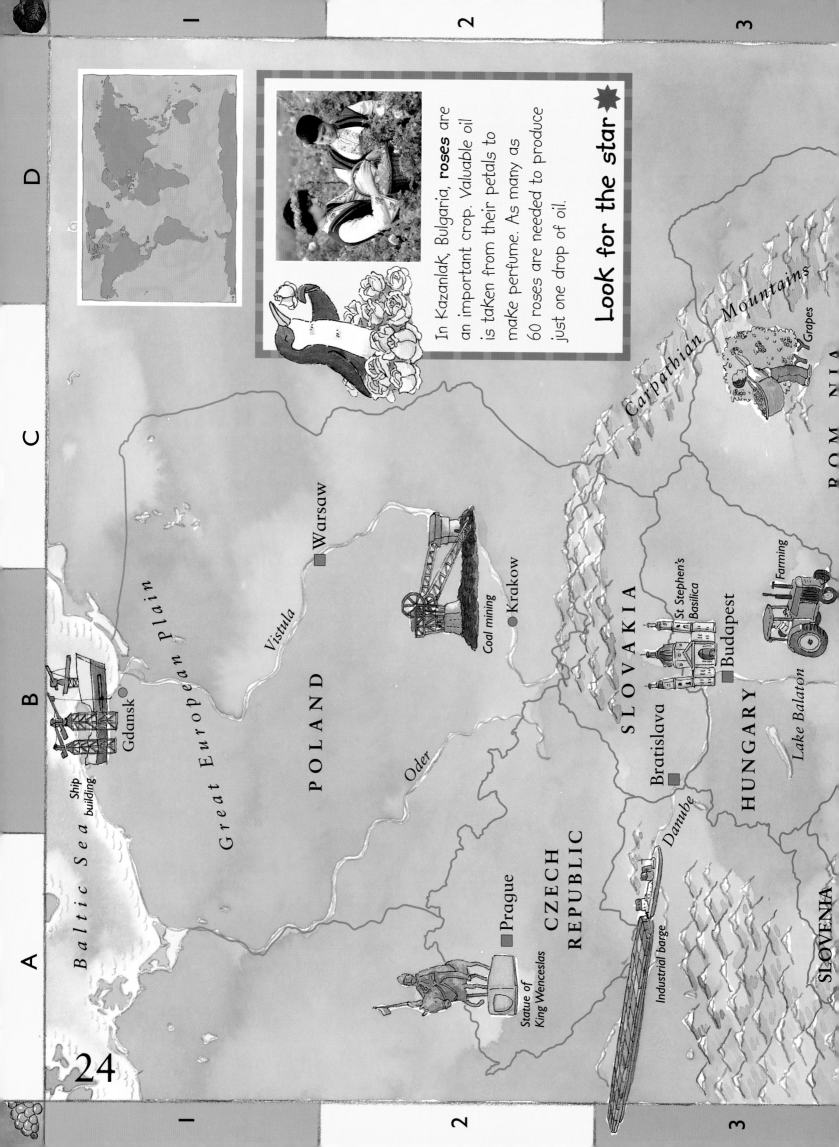

24

A   B   C   D

1   2   3

Baltic Sea

Ship building

Gdansk

Great European Plain

Vistula

Warsaw

POLAND

Coal mining

Krakow

Oder

Prague

CZECH REPUBLIC

Statue of King Wenceslas

Danube

Industrial barge

SLOVAKIA

Bratislava

St Stephen's Basilica

Budapest

HUNGARY

Lake Balaton

Farming

SLOVENIA

Carpathian Mountains

ROMANIA

Grapes

In Kazanlak, Bulgaria, **roses** are an important crop. Valuable oil is taken from their petals to make perfume. As many as 60 roses are needed to produce just one drop of oil.

★ **Look for the star**

Eastern Europe

A lot of eastern Europe is covered with mountains and forests, but people farm the land where they can. Winter is cold in the north, but the south is hotter, with good tourist beaches. There are many different cultures and traditions in the region.

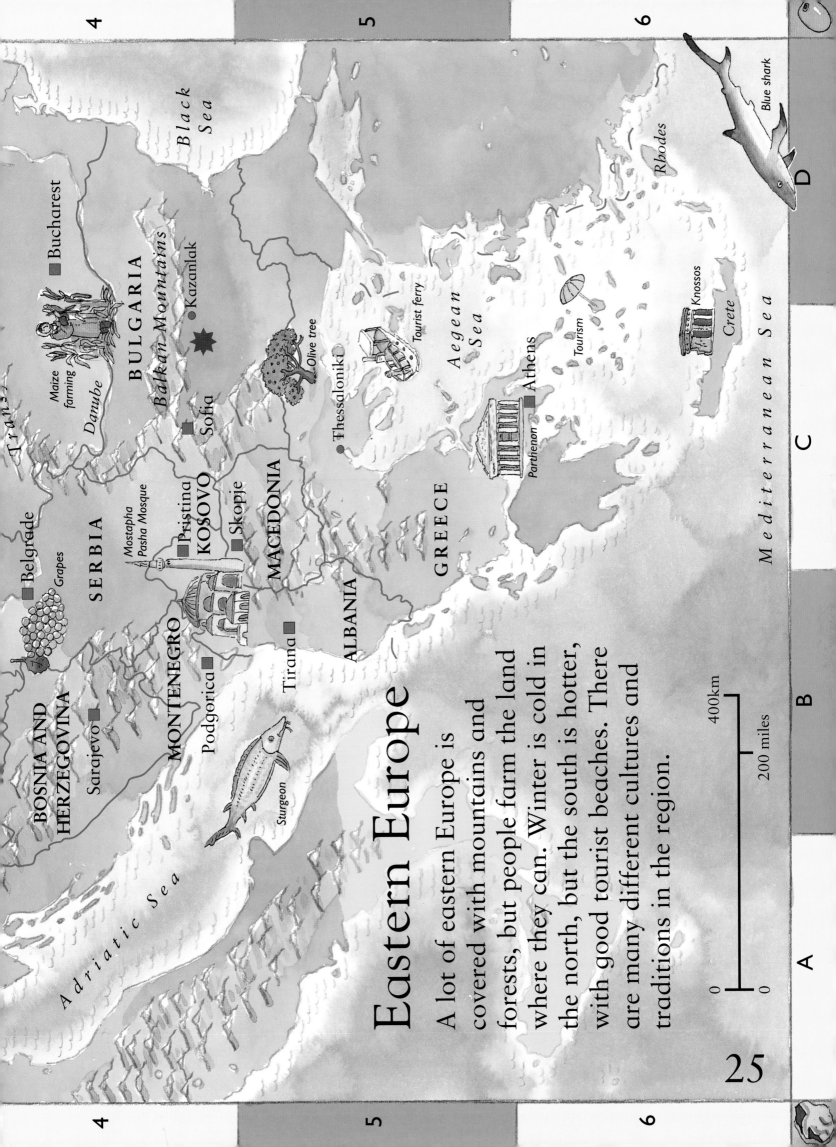

Blue shark

Rhodes

Knossos

Crete

Mediterranean Sea

Black Sea

Bucharest

BULGARIA

Balkan Mountains

Kazanlak

Sofia

Tourist ferry

Aegean Sea

Athens

Parthenon

Tourism

Thessaloniki

Olive tree

Sea

GREECE

MACEDONIA

Skopje

KOSOVO

Pristina

Mostapha Pasha Mosque

SERBIA

Belgrade

Grapes

ALBANIA

Tirana

MONTENEGRO

Podgorica

BOSNIA AND HERZEGOVINA

Sarajevo

Adriatic Sea

Sturgeon

Maize farming

Danube

Trans...

0   200 miles

0   400km

A   B   C   D

4   5   6

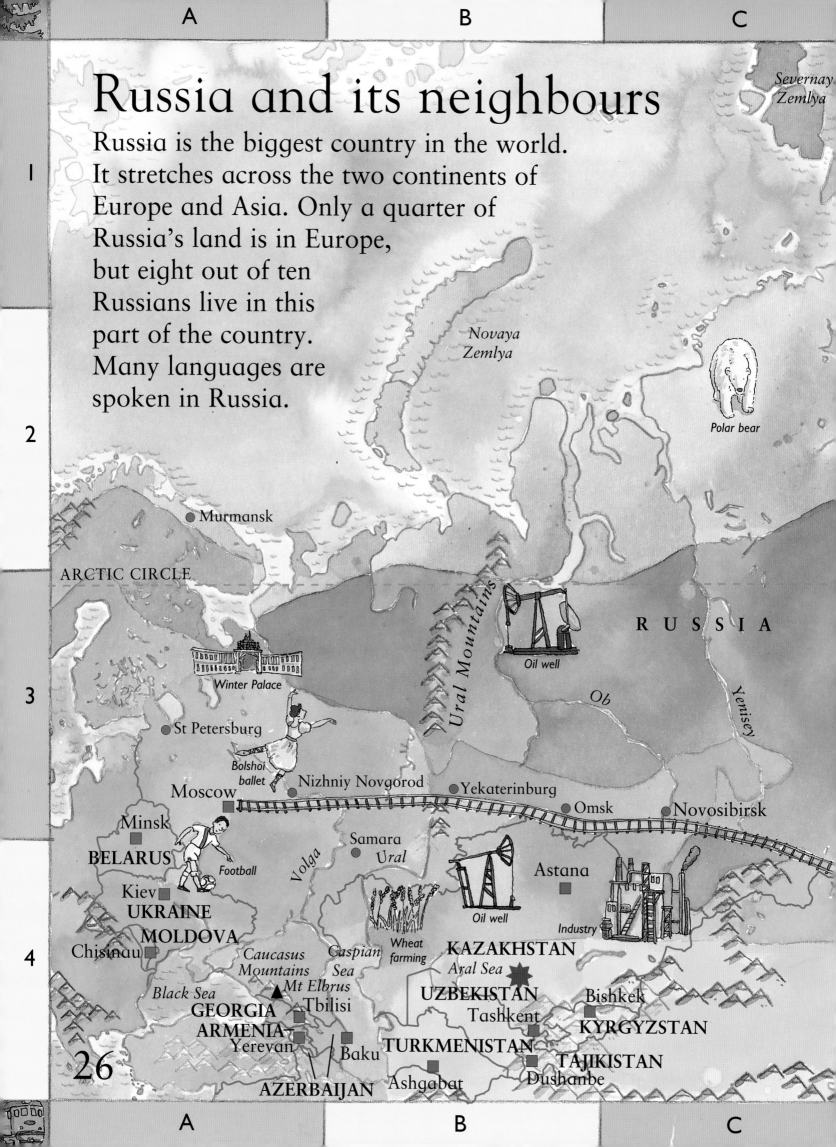

Russia and its neighbours

Russia is the biggest country in the world. It stretches across the two continents of Europe and Asia. Only a quarter of Russia's land is in Europe, but eight out of ten Russians live in this part of the country. Many languages are spoken in Russia.

Severnay Zemlya

Novaya Zemlya

Polar bear

Murmansk

ARCTIC CIRCLE

RUSSIA

Winter Palace

Ural Mountains

Oil well

Ob

Yenisey

St Petersburg

Bolshoi ballet

Moscow

Nizhniy Novgorod

Yekaterinburg

Omsk

Novosibirsk

Minsk

BELARUS

Football

Volga

Samara

Ural

Astana

Kiev

UKRAINE

MOLDOVA

Chisinau

Caucasus Mountains

Caspian Sea

Wheat farming

Oil well

Industry

KAZAKHSTAN

Aral Sea

Black Sea

Mt Elbrus

Tbilisi

UZBEKISTAN

Bishkek

GEORGIA

ARMENIA

Tashkent

KYRGYZSTAN

Yerevan

Baku

TURKMENISTAN

TAJIKISTAN

Ashgabat

Dushanbe

AZERBAIJAN

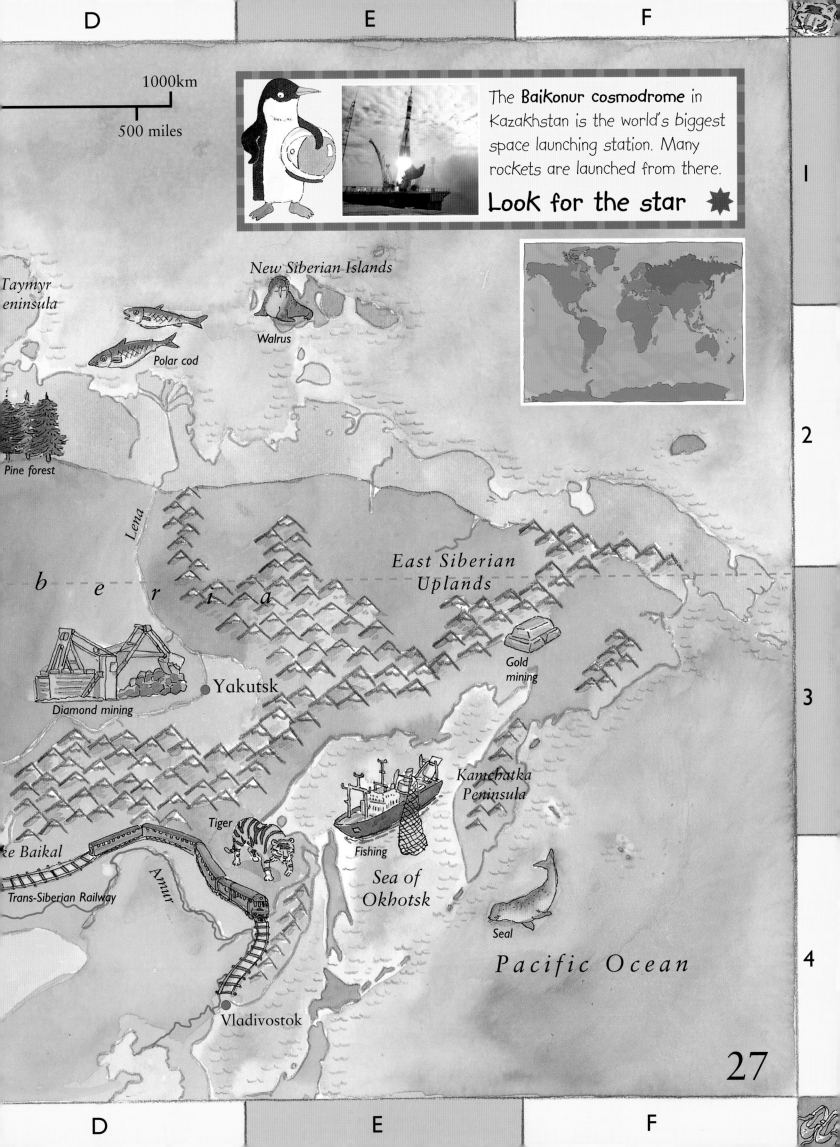

1000km

500 miles

The **Baikonur cosmodrome** in Kazakhstan is the world's biggest space launching station. Many rockets are launched from there.

Look for the star ✴

Taymyr eninsula

New Siberian Islands

Polar cod

Walrus

Pine forest

Lena

b   e   r   i   a

East Siberian Uplands

Gold mining

Diamond mining

● Yakutsk

Kamchatka Peninsula

Tiger

Fishing

Sea of Okhotsk

ke Baikal

Amur

Trans-Siberian Railway

Seal

Pacific Ocean

● Vladivostok

27

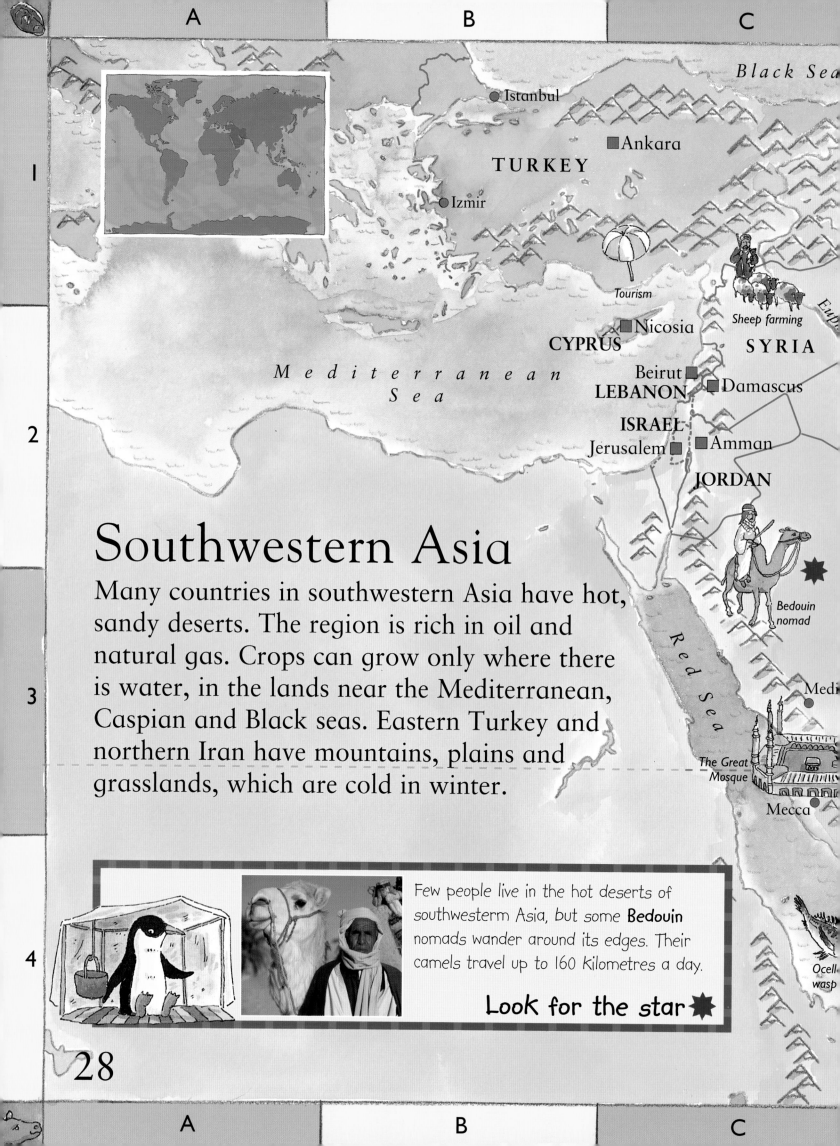

Istanbul

Ankara

TURKEY

Izmir

Black Sea

Tourism

Nicosia

CYPRUS

Sheep farming

SYRIA

Eu...

M e d i t e r r a n e a n
S e a

Beirut
LEBANON

Damascus

ISRAEL
Jerusalem Amman

JORDAN

Southwestern Asia

Many countries in southwestern Asia have hot,
sandy deserts. The region is rich in oil and
natural gas. Crops can grow only where there
is water, in the lands near the Mediterranean,
Caspian and Black seas. Eastern Turkey and
northern Iran have mountains, plains and
grasslands, which are cold in winter.

Bedouin
nomad

R e d   S e a

Medi...

The Great
Mosque

Mecca

Few people live in the hot deserts of
southwestern Asia, but some **Bedouin**
nomads wander around its edges. Their
camels travel up to 160 kilometres a day.

Look for the star ✴

Ocell...
wasp

28

D E F

1

0   800km

0   500 miles

Caspian Sea

Tabriz

Oil rig

Mashhad

osul

Tehran

Onager

Carpet making

I R A N

Baghdad

Tigris

Esfahan

IRAQ

Zagros Mountains

2

Basra

KUWAIT

Kuwait City

Oil refinery

The Gulf

BAHRAIN

Manama

Oil well

OMAN

Oil well

SAUDI ARABIA

Doha

QATAR

Abu Dhabi

Riyadh

U. A. E.

Muscat

3

TROPIC OF CANCER

Arabian Desert

OMAN

*Empty Quarter
(Rub al Khali)*

Dhow

*Arabian
oryx*

*A r a b i a n
S e a*

YEMEN

*Orange-spotted
trevally*

4

Sana

Dates

Gulf of Aden

Aden

29

D E F

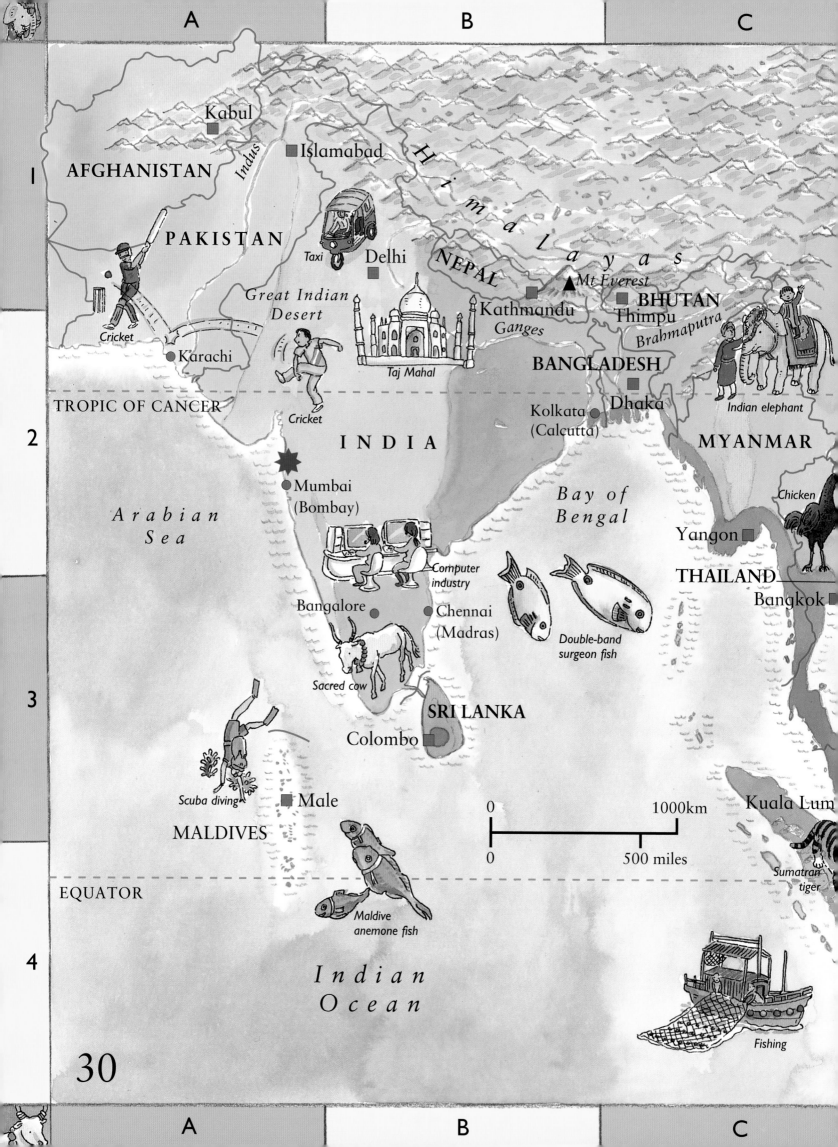

A

B

C

Kabul

Islamabad

AFGHANISTAN

Indus

1

Himalayas

Taxi

Delhi

PAKISTAN

NEPAL

▲ Mt Everest

BHUTAN

Cricket

Kathmandu

Thimpu

Great Indian
Desert

Ganges

Brahmaputra

Karachi

Taj Mahal

BANGLADESH

Indian elephant

TROPIC OF CANCER

Cricket

Dhaka

2

I N D I A

Kolkata
(Calcutta)

MYANMAR

Mumbai
(Bombay)

Bay of
Bengal

Chicken

*A r a b i a n
S e a*

Yangon

Computer
industry

THAILAND

Bangalore

Chennai
(Madras)

Bangkok

Double-band
surgeon fish

Sacred cow

3

SRI LANKA

Scuba diving

Colombo

0   1000km

Kuala Lum

Male

0   500 miles

MALDIVES

Sumatran
tiger

EQUATOR

Maldive
anemone fish

4

*I n d i a n
O c e a n*

Fishing

30

Southern and southeastern Asia

The countries of this region are near the equator, so the weather is very hot. Dusty plains stretch across India. Thick rainforests grow in Malaysia and Indonesia. Most people farm in small villages, or work in big cities. A long mountain range called the Himalayas lies to the north.

The world's biggest movie industry, **Bollywood**, is based in Mumbai (Bombay), India. About 800 new films are made here every year.

Look for the star ✸

VIETNAM

■ Hanoi

OS

ntiane

South China Sea

Mekong

Basket boat

MBODIA

Rice

hnom enh

Oil rig

■ Manila

PHILIPPINES

BRUNEI

Begawan Seri

ALAYSIA

INGAPORE

gapore

Orang utan

Rainforest

I N D O N E S I A

■ Jakarta

■ Dili
EAST TIMOR

31

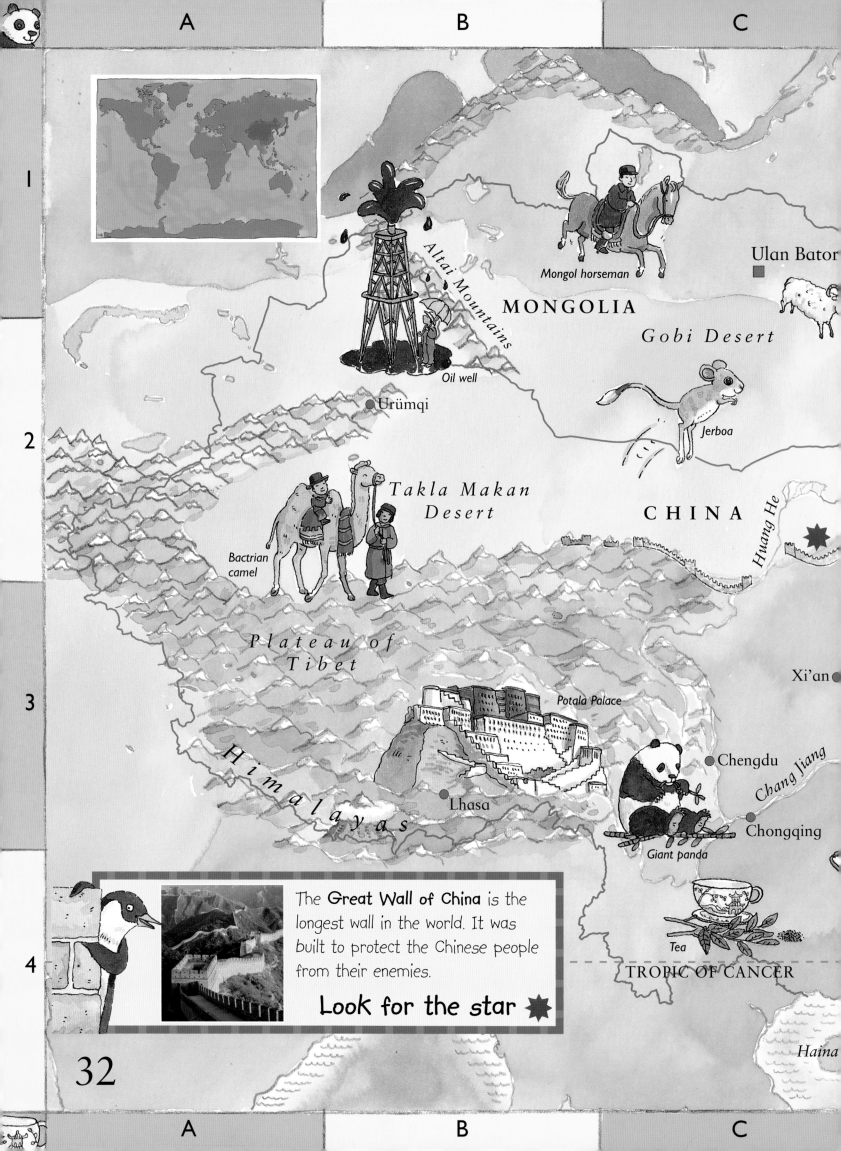

A   B   C

Altai Mountains

Oil well

Mongol horseman

Ulan Bator

MONGOLIA

Gobi Desert

Jerboa

Urümqi

Takla Makan Desert

CHINA

Huang He

Bactrian camel

Plateau of Tibet

Potala Palace

Xi'an

H i m a l a y a s

Chengdu

Chang Jiang

Lhasa

Chongqing

Giant panda

Tea

The **Great Wall of China** is the longest wall in the world. It was built to protect the Chinese people from their enemies.

Look for the star ✶

TROPIC OF CANCER

Haina

32

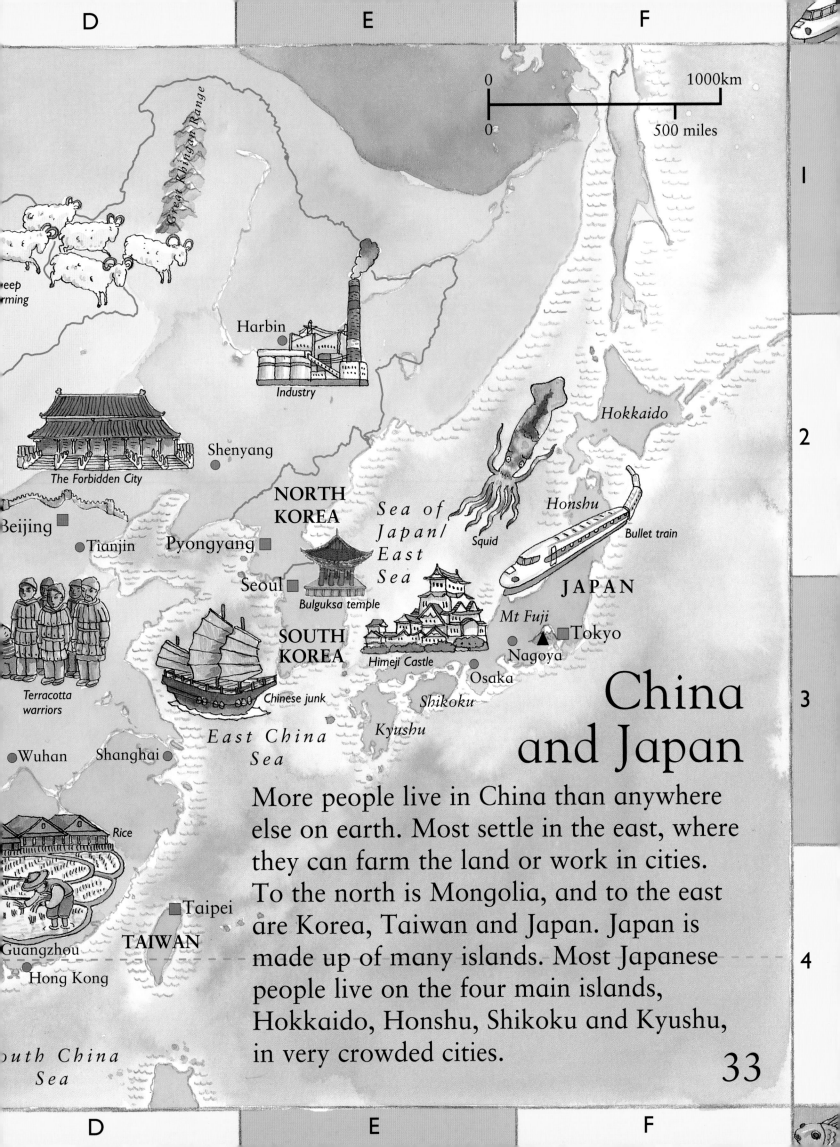

Top labels

D   E   F

0   1000km

0   500 miles

Great Khingan Range

Sheep farming

Harbin

Industry

The Forbidden City

Shenyang

Hokkaido

Honshu

Squid

Bullet train

NORTH KOREA

Sea of Japan/ East Sea

Beijing

Tianjin

Pyongyang

Seoul

Bulguksa temple

JAPAN

Mt Fuji

Tokyo

Nagoya

SOUTH KOREA

Himeji Castle

Osaka

Terracotta warriors

Chinese junk

Shikoku

East China Sea

Kyushu

Wuhan   Shanghai

Rice

Taipei

TAIWAN

Guangzhou

Hong Kong

South China Sea

China and Japan

More people live in China than anywhere else on earth. Most settle in the east, where they can farm the land or work in cities. To the north is Mongolia, and to the east are Korea, Taiwan and Japan. Japan is made up of many islands. Most Japanese people live on the four main islands, Hokkaido, Honshu, Shikoku and Kyushu, in very crowded cities.

33

I   2   3   4

D   E   F

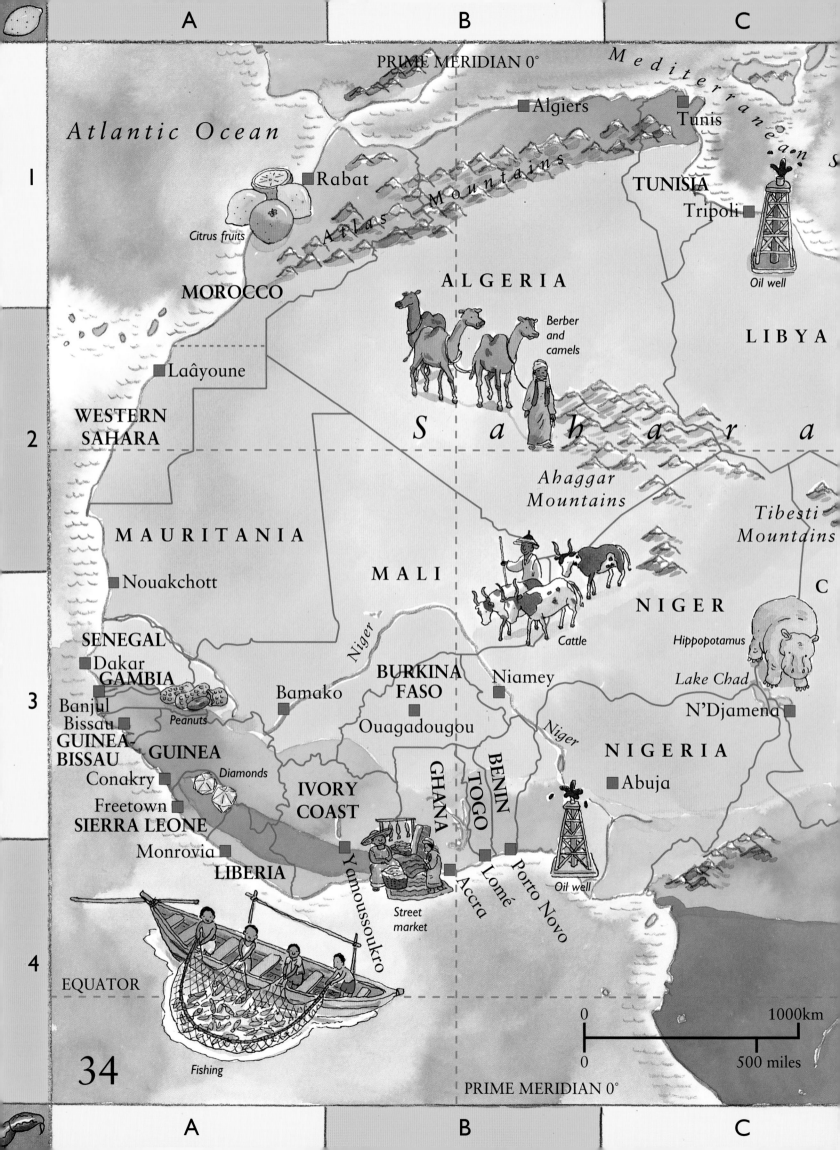

A B C

PRIME MERIDIAN 0°

Mediterranean S

Atlantic Ocean

Algiers

Tunis

1

Rabat

TUNISIA

Citrus fruits

Tripoli

A L G E R I A

LIBYA

MOROCCO

Oil well

Laâyoune

Berber and camels

2

WESTERN SAHARA

S a h a r a

Ahaggar Mountains

Tibesti Mountains

M A U R I T A N I A

Nouakchott

M A L I

C

N I G E R

Hippopotamus

Lake Chad

Niger

SENEGAL

Dakar

GAMBIA

BURKINA

Niamey

N'Djamena

3

Banjul

Bamako

FASO

Bissau

Peanuts

Ouagadougou

Niger

N I G E R I A

GUINEA-BISSAU

GUINEA

Diamonds

GHANA

BENIN

Abuja

Conakry

IVORY COAST

TOGO

Freetown

Cattle

SIERRA LEONE

Monrovia

Lomé

Oil well

Porto Novo

LIBERIA

Yamoussoukro

Accra

Street market

4

EQUATOR

Fishing

0 _____ 1000km

0 _____ 500 miles

34

PRIME MERIDIAN 0°

A B C

1

Northern Africa

The Sahara is the world's biggest desert. It stretches across the whole of northern Africa. Most people live south of the Sahara or near the coast. The world's longest river, the Nile, flows from central Africa, through Egypt to the Mediterranean Sea.

TROPIC OF CANCER

2

■ Cairo

E G Y P T

Tutankhamun's funerary mask

Scorpion

Lake Nasser

Red Sea

Cotton plant

D

Nile

Crocodile

ERITREA

■ Khartoum

■ Asmara

S U D A N

Ethiopian Highlands

DJIBOUTI

3

■ Addis Ababa

E T H I O P I A

Starry triggerfish

SOMALIA

■ Mogadishu

4

The **pyramids**, near Cairo in Egypt, were built over 4,000 years ago. They are the largest stone buildings in the world.

Look for the star ✴

Indian Ocean

35

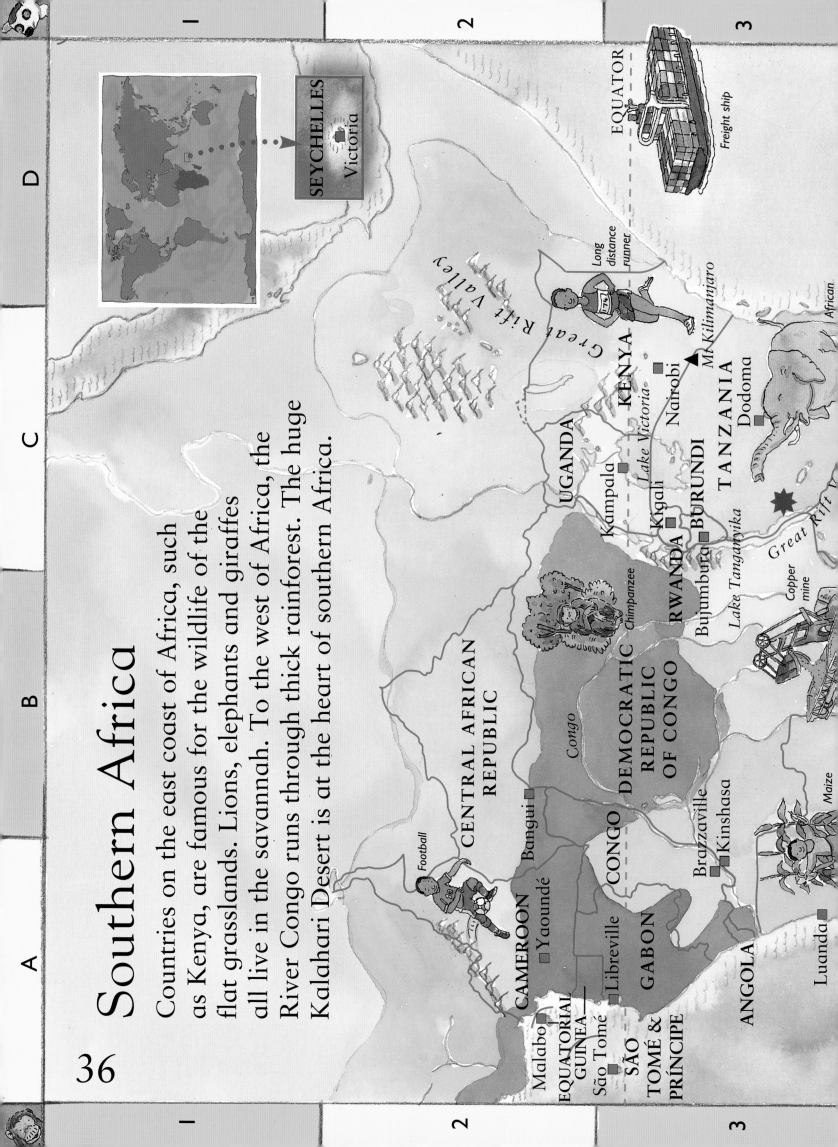

Southern Africa

Countries on the east coast of Africa, such as Kenya, are famous for the wildlife of the flat grasslands. Lions, elephants and giraffes all live in the savannah. To the west of Africa, the River Congo runs through thick rainforest. The huge Kalahari Desert is at the heart of southern Africa.

SEYCHELLES
Victoria

EQUATOR

Freight ship

Long distance runner

Great Rift Valley

UGANDA

Kampala

KENYA

Lake Victoria

Nairobi

Mt Kilimanjaro

RWANDA
Kigali

BURUNDI
Bujumbura

TANZANIA

Dodoma

Chimpanzee

Lake Tanganyika

Great Rift V

Copper mine

African

CENTRAL AFRICAN REPUBLIC

Congo

DEMOCRATIC REPUBLIC OF CONGO

CONGO

Brazzaville

Kinshasa

Football

CAMEROON
Yaoundé

Bangui

EQUATORIAL GUINEA
Malabo

SÃO TOMÉ & PRÍNCIPE
São Tomé

Libreville

GABON

ANGOLA

Luanda

Maize

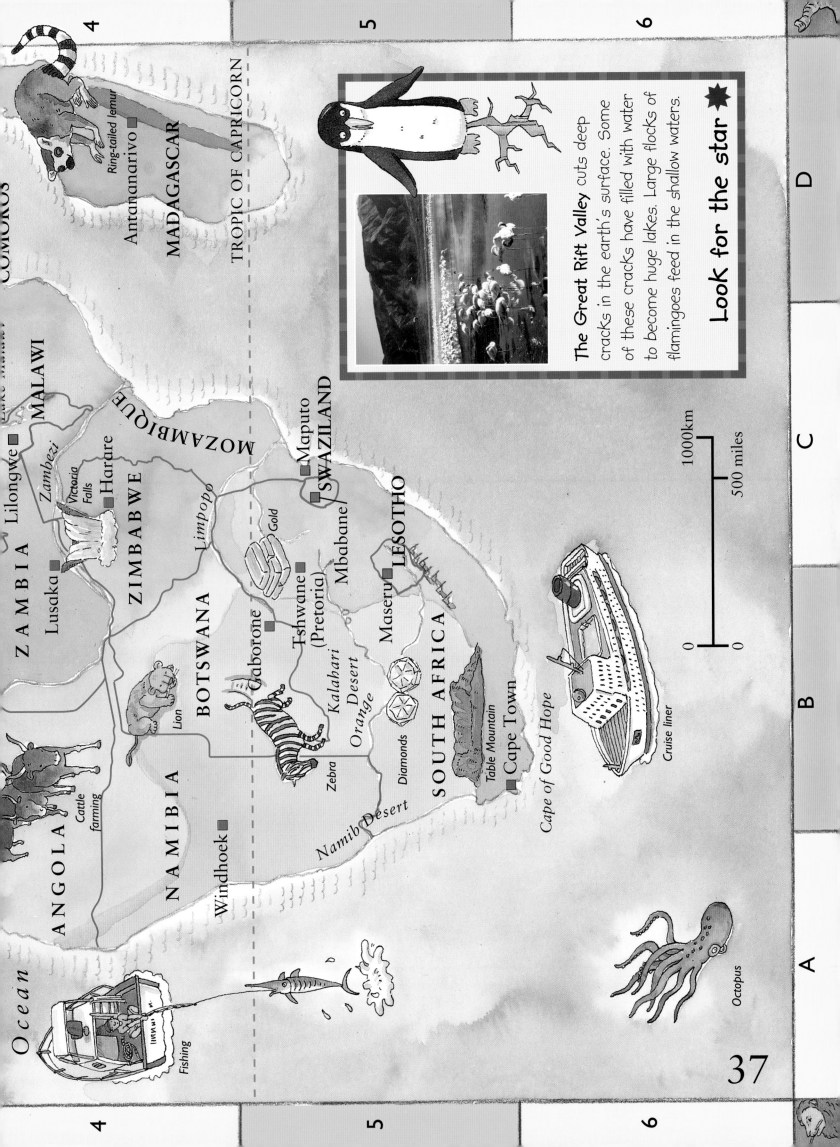

Ocean

COMOROS

4

Ring-tailed lemur

Antananarivo

MADAGASCAR

TROPIC OF CAPRICORN

MALAWI

Lilongwe

Zambezi

MOZAMBIQUE

Victoria Falls

Harare

ZIMBABWE

Lusaka

ZAMBIA

ANGOLA

Cattle farming

Lion

NAMIBIA

BOTSWANA

Limpopo

Gaborone

Gold

Windhoek

Zebra

Kalahari Desert

Orange

Namib Desert

Maputo

SWAZILAND

Tshwane (Pretoria)

Mbabane

Maseru

LESOTHO

Diamonds

SOUTH AFRICA

Table Mountain

Cape Town

Cape of Good Hope

Fishing

Octopus

Cruise liner

The Great Rift Valley cuts deep cracks in the earth's surface. Some of these cracks have filled with water to become huge lakes. Large flocks of flamingoes feed in the shallow waters.

★ Look for the star

0   500 miles

0   1000km

5

6

A   B   C   D

37

1

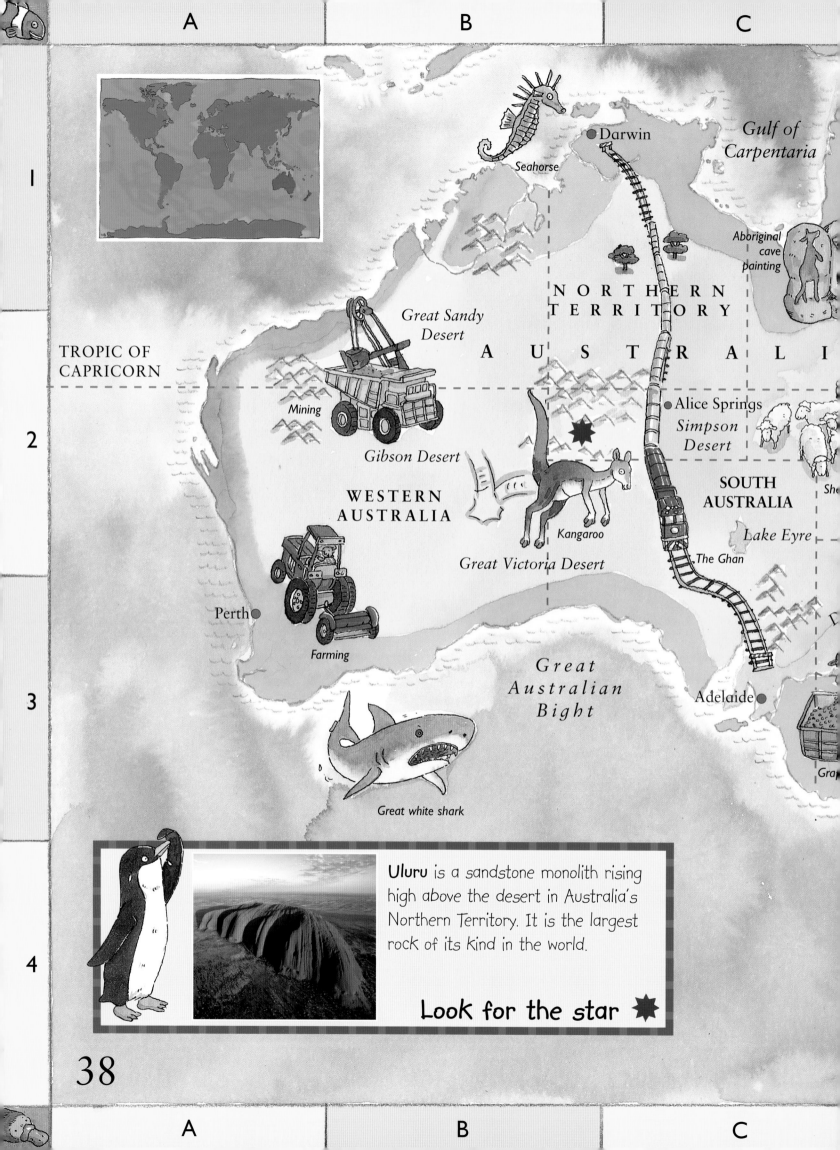

Gulf of
Carpentaria

Darwin

Seahorse

Aboriginal
cave
painting

N O R T H E R N
T E R R I T O R Y

A U S T R A L I

TROPIC OF
CAPRICORN

Great Sandy
Desert

2

Mining

Gibson Desert

Alice Springs
Simpson
Desert

SOUTH
AUSTRALIA

She

WESTERN
AUSTRALIA

Kangaroo

Lake Eyre

Great Victoria Desert

The Ghan

Perth

Farming

Great
Australian
Bight

3

Adelaide

Gra

Great white shark

Uluru is a sandstone monolith rising
high above the desert in Australia's
Northern Territory. It is the largest
rock of its kind in the world.

4

Look for the star ✦

Australia and New Zealand

Australia is the only country that is also a continent. In the centre of Australia there are many deserts. To the north are tropical rainforests. Most Australian people live in cities by the sea.

New Zealand is 1,600km from Australia. It is a land of mountains and glaciers. Like Australia, it has many sheep and cattle farms.

Coral Sea

Clown fish

Dividing Range

Pacific Ocean

QUEENSLAND   ● Brisbane

Duck-billed platypus

NEW SOUTH WALES

Sydney ●   Sydney Opera House

Red snapper fish

Rugby

NORTH ISLAND

■ Canberra
AUSTRALIAN CAPITAL TERRITORY

Murray

NEW ZEALAND

● Auckland

● Hamilton

VICTORIA

Melbourne

Surfing

Lake Taupo

Bass Strait

Tasmanian devil

Tasman Sea

Kiwi

■ Wellington

● Hobart

SOUTH ISLAND

TASMANIA

Southern Alps

Mt Cook ▲   ● Christchurch

Fishing

1000km

● Dunedin

500 miles

Yellow-fin fish

39

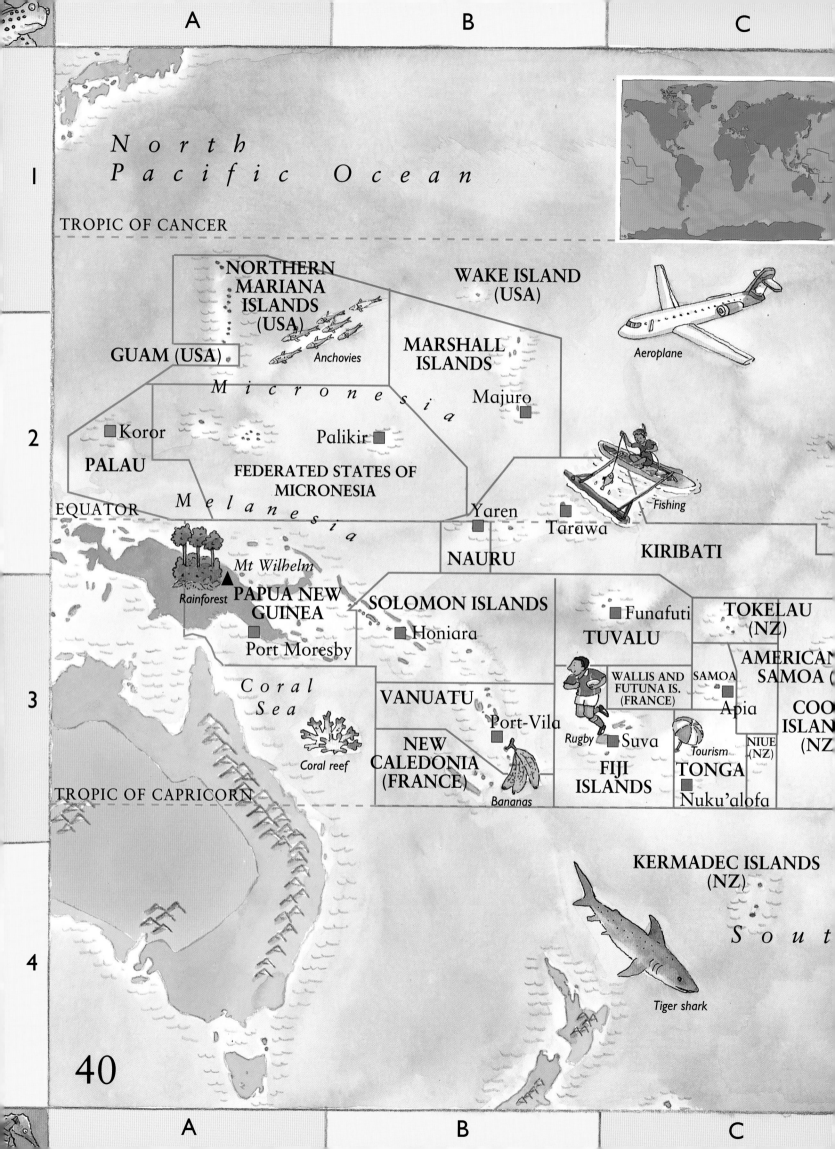

North Pacific Ocean

TROPIC OF CANCER

NORTHERN MARIANA ISLANDS (USA)

WAKE ISLAND (USA)

GUAM (USA)

Anchovies

Aeroplane

MARSHALL ISLANDS

Micronesia

Majuro

■ Koror

Palikir ■

PALAU

FEDERATED STATES OF MICRONESIA

Fishing

Melanesia

EQUATOR

Yaren ■

Tarawa

Mt Wilhelm

NAURU

KIRIBATI

▲

Rainforest

PAPUA NEW GUINEA

SOLOMON ISLANDS

Funafuti ■

TOKELAU (NZ)

Honiara ■

TUVALU

■ Port Moresby

Coral Sea

AMERICAN SAMOA

VANUATU

WALLIS AND FUTUNA IS. (FRANCE)

SAMOA ■

Apia

Coral reef

Port-Vila ■

Rugby ■ Suva

Tourism

COOK ISLANDS (NZ)

NEW CALEDONIA (FRANCE)

NIUE (NZ)

FIJI ISLANDS

TONGA ■

TROPIC OF CAPRICORN

Bananas

Nuku'alofa

KERMADEC ISLANDS (NZ)

Sout

Tiger shark

40

The Pacific Islands

There are thousands of islands in the Pacific Ocean. All these islands, with Australia, New Zealand and Papua New Guinea, make up a region called Oceania. Many Pacific islanders live in communities that have little contact with the rest of the world. Some of their traditions have not changed for centuries.

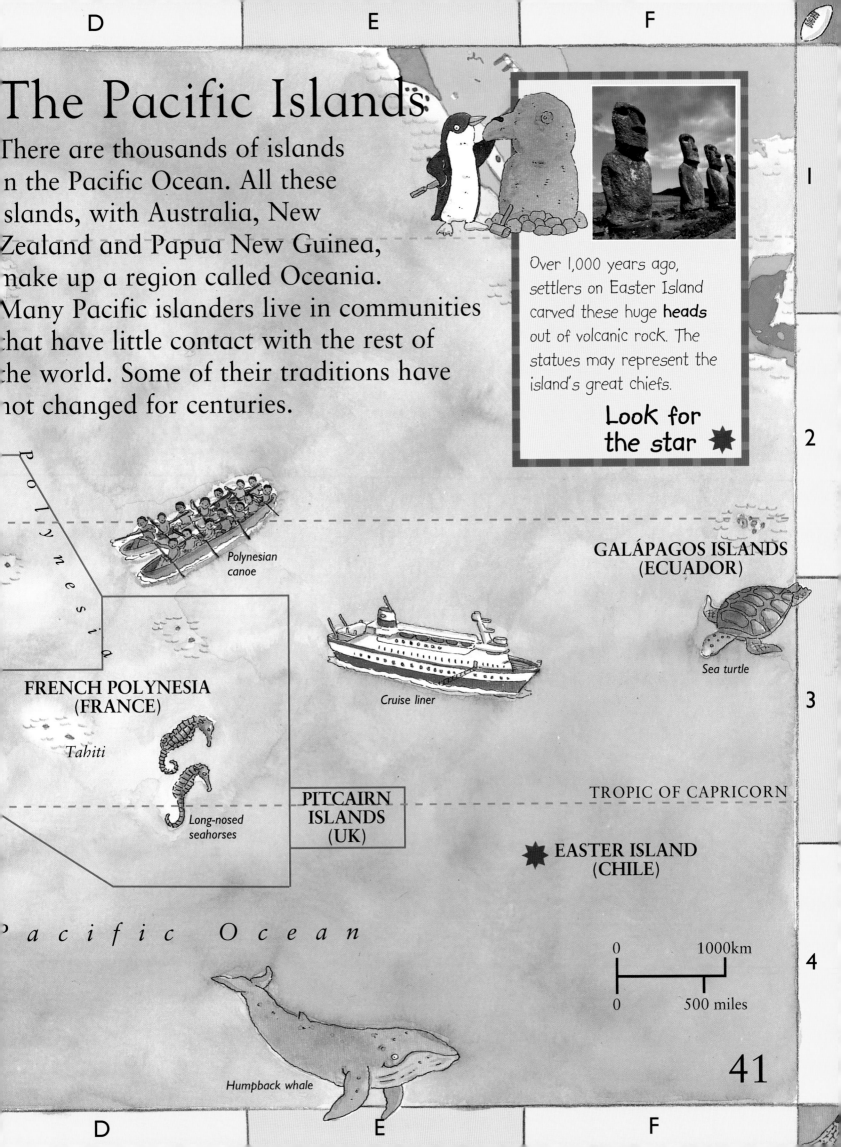

Over 1,000 years ago, settlers on Easter Island carved these huge **heads** out of volcanic rock. The statues may represent the island's great chiefs.

Look for the star ✸

Polynesian canoe

Cruise liner

GALÁPAGOS ISLANDS (ECUADOR)

Sea turtle

FRENCH POLYNESIA (FRANCE)

Tahiti

Long-nosed seahorses

PITCAIRN ISLANDS (UK)

TROPIC OF CAPRICORN

✸ **EASTER ISLAND (CHILE)**

P a c i f i c   O c e a n

P o l y n e s i a

0   1000km

0   500 miles

Humpback whale

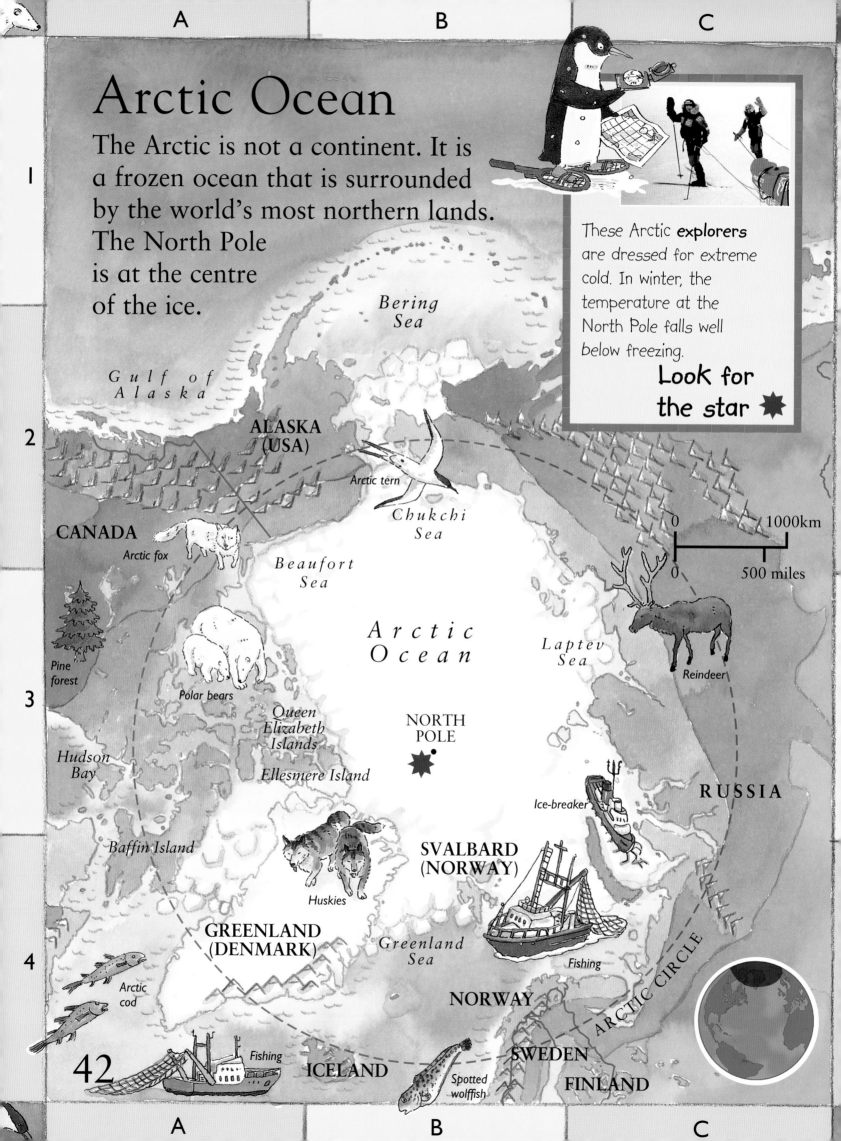

Arctic Ocean

The Arctic is not a continent. It is a frozen ocean that is surrounded by the world's most northern lands. The North Pole is at the centre of the ice.

These Arctic **explorers** are dressed for extreme cold. In winter, the temperature at the North Pole falls well below freezing.

Look for the star ✦

Bering Sea

Gulf of Alaska

ALASKA (USA)

Arctic tern

Chukchi Sea

CANADA

Arctic fox

Beaufort Sea

0   1000km

0   500 miles

A r c t i c O c e a n

Laptev Sea

Pine forest

Polar bears

Reindeer

Queen Elizabeth Islands

NORTH POLE ✦

Hudson Bay

Ellesmere Island

Ice-breaker

RUSSIA

Baffin Island

Huskies

SVALBARD (NORWAY)

GREENLAND (DENMARK)

Greenland Sea

Fishing

Arctic cod

NORWAY

ARCTIC CIRCLE

42

Fishing

ICELAND

Spotted wolffish

SWEDEN

FINLAND

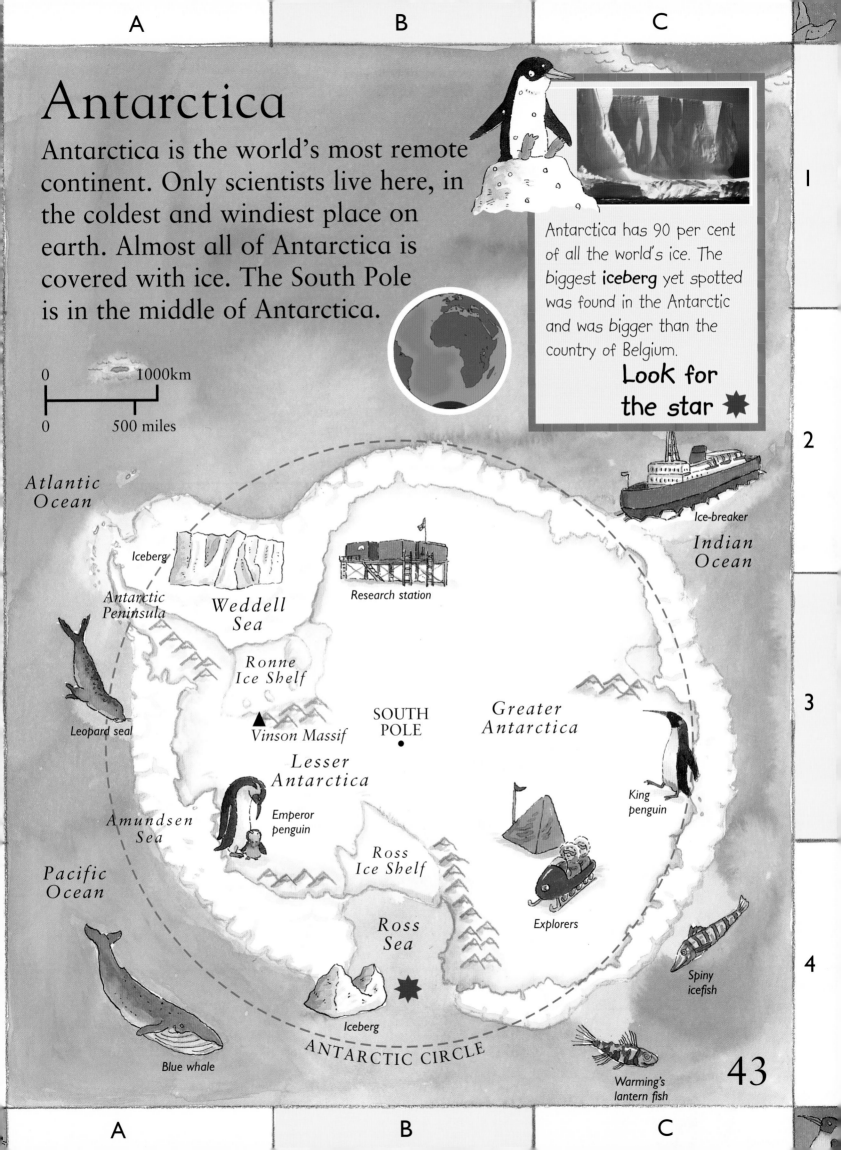

Antarctica

Antarctica is the world's most remote continent. Only scientists live here, in the coldest and windiest place on earth. Almost all of Antarctica is covered with ice. The South Pole is in the middle of Antarctica.

0   1000km

0   500 miles

Antarctica has 90 per cent of all the world's ice. The biggest **iceberg** yet spotted was found in the Antarctic and was bigger than the country of Belgium.

Look for the star ✦

Atlantic Ocean

Iceberg

Antarctic Peninsula

Weddell Sea

Research station

Ice-breaker

Indian Ocean

Leopard seal

Ronne Ice Shelf

▲
Vinson Massif

SOUTH POLE

Greater Antarctica

King penguin

Lesser Antarctica

Emperor penguin

Amundsen Sea

Explorers

Pacific Ocean

Ross Ice Shelf

Ross Sea

Iceberg ✦

Spiny icefish

ANTARCTIC CIRCLE

Blue whale

Warming's lantern fish

1

ARCTIC CIRCLE

Fishing

Blue whale

Deep sea submersible

Car ferry

2

TROPIC OF CANCER

Oil rig

Cruise liner

Scuba diving

Caribbean Sea

Atlantic Ocean

Fishing

EQUATOR

Pacific Ocean

Freight ship

TROPIC OF CAPRICORN

3

Fishing

The oceans

Seen from space, the earth looks blue. This is because almost three quarters of the planet is covered with water. The earth has four great oceans, the Pacific, Atlantic, Indian and Arctic oceans. The Pacific is the biggest of these oceans.

Oil rig

4

Factory fishing ship

Iceberg

PRIME MERIDIAN

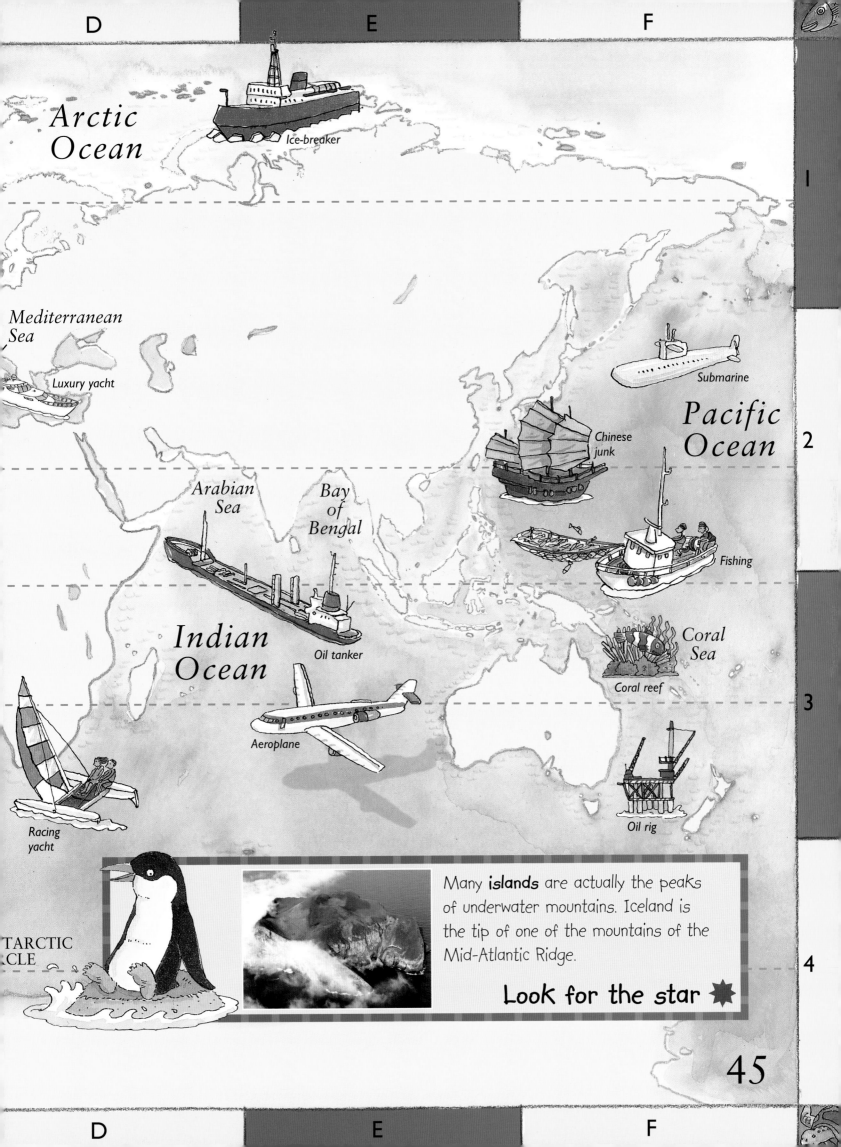

D E F

1

Arctic Ocean

Ice-breaker

Mediterranean Sea

Luxury yacht

Submarine

Pacific Ocean

2

Chinese junk

Arabian Sea

Bay of Bengal

Fishing

Indian Ocean

Oil tanker

Coral Sea

Coral reef

3

Aeroplane

Racing yacht

Oil rig

ANTARCTIC CLE

Many **islands** are actually the peaks of underwater mountains. Iceland is the tip of one of the mountains of the Mid-Atlantic Ridge.

4

Look for the star ✸

45

D E F

Index

47